Dedicated to the memory of E. Roy Smith,
former Parry Sound mayor and MPP,
who first suggested to me that the deeds of
Francis Pegahmagabow should not remain forgotten

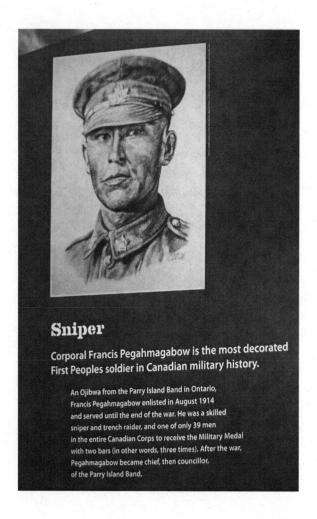

Sniper

Corporal Francis Pegahmagabow is the most decorated First Peoples soldier in Canadian military history.

An Ojibwa from the Parry Island Band in Ontario,
Francis Pegahmagabow enlisted in August 1914
and served until the end of the war. He was a skilled
sniper and trench raider, and one of only 39 men
in the entire Canadian Corps to receive the Military Medal
with two bars (in other words, three times). After the war,
Pegahmagabow became chief, then councillor,
of the Parry Island Band.

Part of the permanent display, Canadian War Museum, Ottawa, acknowledging the military exploits of Corporal Francis Pegahmagabow.

Pegahmagabow

LIFE-LONG WARRIOR

ADRIAN HAYES

Foreword by
HON. JAMES BARTLEMAN

Blue Butterfly Books
THINK FREE, BE FREE

Blue Butterfly Book Publishing Inc.
2583 Lakeshore Boulevard West, Toronto, Ontario, Canada M8V 1G3
Tel 416-255-3930   Fax 416-252-8291   www.bluebutterflybooks.ca

Complete ordering information for Blue Butterfly titles is available at:
www.bluebutterflybooks.ca

Originally published in 2003 by Fox Meadow Creations
First Blue Butterfly edition, soft cover: 2009

Library and Archives Canada Cataloguing in Publication

Hayes, Adrian
Pegahmagabow : life-long warrior / Adrian Hayes ; foreword by
James Bartleman.

Includes bibliographical references and index.
ISBN 978-0-9784982-9-0

1. Pegahmagabow, Francis, 1889–1952. 2. Canada. Canadian
Army. Canadian Expeditionary Force—Biography. 3. Indian
veterans—Canada—Biography. 4. Indian activists—Canada—Biography.
5. Ojibwa Indians—Ontario—Parry Sound Region—Biography. i. Title.

E99.C6H38 2009   971.004'9730092   C2009-900952-8

Design, typesetting and maps by Gary Long / Fox Meadow Creations
Text set in Tyrnavia, maps in Myriad
Printed and bound in Canada by Transcontinental-Métrolitho

The text paper in this book, Rolland Enviro 100 from Cascades, contains 100 per cent post-consumer recycled fibre, was processed chlorine free, and was manufactured using energy from biogas recovered from a municipal landfill site and piped to the mill.

*Blue Butterfly Books thanks book buyers for their support
in the marketplace.*

Contents

When James Bartleman became Ontario's first aboriginal lieutenant-governor, he knew only too well the conditions faced by Francis Pegah-magabow. His Honour used the full powers of his often-ceremonial position to achieve real results for First Nations' children in isolated northern reserves and was asked by Premier Dalton McGuinty, in a rare event, to address the Ontario Legislature about this initiative. On his visits to these First Nation communities to oversee his program of distributing free books to youngsters in places lacking a library, he delighted, as captured in this photo, to engage and inspire children.

Out from the Shadows

BY HON. JAMES BARTLEMAN

THE LIVES OF OTHERS can teach us a lot about our own.

In this story of a Canadian aboriginal, who out of patriotism was a warrior for his country in time of global war and then out of necessity became a warrior for his human rights in time of peace, we discover truths about ourselves, both individually and as a society collectively. The discoveries are not particularly comforting.

Adrian Hayes, author of this biography of Corporal Francis Pegahmagabow, first learned about the story of Canada's most-decorated First Peoples soldier when he was a reporter in his hometown of Parry Sound, writing a column on local history in the *North Star*. Parry Sound is near a reserve known today as the Wasauksing First Nation, on Parry Island, where Francis Pegahmagabow lived.

Although traditionally a nomadic people who moved west towards Georgian Bay in the spring to fish and farther inland to hunting grounds in the fall, Pegahmagabow's Ojibwa ancestors by the 1830s resided at the village of Obajewanung (on the site of present-day Port Carling, where I grew up), living in log cabins and cultivating potatoes, corn, and other crops. Chief James Pegahmagabow Sr. tried to have a reserve proclaimed in this area, but with the launching of the steamship *Wenonah* on Lake Muskoka and the arrival of settlers eager to claim the land, the first inhabitants were forced to relocate in the 1860s to Parry Island, a rocky, inhospitable island of 18,500 acres in Georgian Bay that had been set aside as a reserve by an 1853 order in council.* Here these valiant people had no choice but to return to the hand-to-mouth existence of their forebears, living in tents and relying on hunting and fishing rather than on agriculture for survival. Meanwhile, the graves of their ancestors were ploughed over, the name Obajewanung forgotten, and the long narrative of what had recently been the most important First Nation community in Muskoka was studiously ignored when the history of early settlement in the district was published.

Such an eclipse of the true story is a well-known Canadian phenomenon. The long-neglected account of the adventures and setbacks of Francis Pegahmagabow is an integral part of this "out of sight, out of mind" mentality. Its dark underside is a constant through Canadian history. In the Second World War, during the harsh battle for Ortona in Italy in late 1943, as Adrian Hayes recounts in this book, Lance-Sergeant Joseph Flavien St. Germain, a Cree from northern Alberta, was told by his commanding officer, "What a magnificent job you've done in the fighting,

*At Parry Island the original residents of Obajewanung, known to what was then the Indian Department as the Muskoka band, joined another group of displaced Ojibwa. The Isle au Sable band had been residing at the nearby mouth of the Seguin River on a 16-square-mile reserve established by the Robinson Huron Treaty of 1850. It was forced to relocate to Parry Island when brothers William M. Gibson and James A. Gibson built a sawmill at a falls near the mouth of the Seguin to work two 50-square-mile timber berths granted in April 1856 by the Crown Lands Department (the mill on the Seguin was the starting point of the town of Parry Sound). In 1877 a group of Potawatomi from Wisconsin also requested to live at Parry Island. Several Odawa families from Michigan arrived at some point before 1884. Before reaching Parry Island, the Potawatomi and Odawa had resided for a number of years at Christian Island farther south in Georgian Bay.

Joe." The soldier looked up and bitterly replied: "It's fine, sir, but if I get back to Canada, I'll be treated just like another poor goddam Indian." He knew what he was talking about. In 1953, when word reached Canada's southern white world that aboriginal people were starving to death in the James Bay region, Prime Minister Louis St. Laurent, head of the Government of Canada which had clear responsibility for Indian affairs, lamented in shock, "We have been governing these people in a state of benign neglect."

To describe neglect as "benign" implies that the injustice and human suffering can somehow be excused, that it was not intentional or premeditated by those currently in office. So while many aboriginal people died, no heads rolled in the Government of Canada. Accountability has not been the strong suit of the Canadian political system. Getting the reality of Canada's "third world conditions" onto the radar screen for mainstream society and the country's political leadership has taken a long time. Only in 2008 did the cultural and human travesty of the residential schools program that separated aboriginal children from their parents and communities earn an apology from the Government of Canada under Prime Minister Stephen Harper, even as the details of compensation remain to be settled. The great strength of this book is that we see, not the overview at a generalized level of abstraction, but the details that paint an exact portrait of the human experience in this context of Canadian apartheid.

From early in this twenty-first century, it is good to be able to look back on the life of Francis Pegahmagabow. From this perspective we can see patterns in history, as well as the details of one man's life and troubled times. That he was heroic in combat during the Great War was consistent with a long tradition of First Nation warriors putting their skills and courage to the test in supporting the British cause in armed conflict. The Chippewas (Ojibwa) from this part of the province, together with other native peoples in what would eventually be called Canada, alongside waves of Indian warriors from the Ohio Valley under Tecumseh, fought on the side of the British in the War of 1812. History records how native intervention at the start of the war prevented the Americans from conquering the British colony. A number of them emerged as decorated war heroes. Their descendents' blood flowed through the veins of Francis Pegahmagabow, and still flows through mine.

Just as consistent, however, as we can also see by taking the long view, was how aboriginals were neglected after the battles had all been won. When honour and victory should have meant more for the First Nations sacrifices, these people were again consigned to the shadows. Who cannot see the pattern of exploitation, calling for help when it was needed but forgetting those who provided it once the crisis had passed? The story of Canadian aboriginals, eclipsed time and again in this manner, has been lived in the shadows and at the margins. Life can be beautiful there, in its own way, again as I know personally—but that existence in the shadows is not a place of justice, equality, health, or prosperity.

Many Canadians, and many people beyond our borders too, whether or not they be aboriginal, will find inspiration in Francis Pegahmagabow's story. His quest shows that vaunted principles of justice, equality, and the rule of law expressed through words in constitutional documents and statutes only take on meaning to the extent they are real in daily places and individual lives. As his life showed, whether as a warrior in armed combat or as a warrior in civilian struggles in the war's long aftermath, one soldier may not win the whole war, but his determination to stand his ground and not to yield is how he helped, in his own moment and opportunity, to turn the tide.

Today we can see, as Pegahmagabow's story comes out from the shadows in this fine book by Adrian Hayes, how much all of us are indebted to him.

Introduction

ALTHOUGH OVERWHELMED by the cheering crowd of over 50,000, Corporal Francis Pegahmagabow felt a surge of intense pride as Edward, the Prince of Wales, pinned several decorations to his chest and shook his hand. That day of pomp and pageantry in August 1919, when close to 200 First World War veterans were recognized at the Canadian National Exhibition for their valour on the battlefields of Europe, was one that he would never forget, because afterwards he ceased being treated as an equal and went back to simply being an Indian.

During the four years he spent wallowing in the mud at places such as Ypres, Givenchy, Cambrai, and Passchendaele, Pegahmagabow had been respected by his fellow soldiers, who depended upon him for his abilities as a scout and sniper. Race and colour mattered little in the trenches where men relied upon each other to stay alive from one horrifying battle to the next. But things were different back in Canada, as Pegahmagabow soon learned.

With the Military Medal and two bars, Pegahmagabow remains the most decorated native soldier in Canadian history, surpassing in gallantry awards Alberta Cree Private Henry Norwest, MM and bar; Sergeant Charles Byce, DCM and MM, of Webbwood, Ontario; and even the legendary Sergeant Tommy Prince, MM and U.S. Silver Star, of Manitoba's Brokenhead band. And while there were some 12,345 Military Medals and 838 first bars awarded to Canadian soldiers during the First World War, only thirty-nine Canadians have ever been recognized with a second bar.

There is a story that during a lull in the terrible struggle for Ortona in Italy at Christmastime 1943, Major Jim Stone of the Loyal Edmonton Regiment remarked to Lance-Sergeant Joseph Flavien St. Germain: "What a magnificent job you've done in the fighting, Joe." St. Germain, a Cree from Dixonville in northern Alberta, looked up and bitterly replied: "It's fine, sir, but if I get back to Canada, I'll be treated just like another poor goddamn Indian."[1] And so it had been for Pegahmagabow after the First World War.

Despite his battlefield heroics, when Pegahmagabow applied repeatedly for a loan under the Soldier Settlement Act of 1919, he was denied because his local Indian agent advised, "I am sure he will never make a farmer and to encourage him to take out a loan for that purpose is only making trouble for himself and the Department in the future."[2] In August 1922, the same agent counselled his superiors against authorizing a $300 loan from band funds so Pegahmagabow could purchase a team of horses, even though by this point he had cleared 10 acres by hand and built a stable. "I do not feel like taking responsibility for the unfortunate animals that might be put in his care if this loan is granted," the agent wrote.[3]

Relegated to a life of severe hardship and near-poverty on the Parry Island reserve during the 1920s and 1930s, Pegahmagabow became increasingly bitter about the control the paternalistic Department of Indian Affairs wielded over the lives of natives. Frequently, he clashed with the Indian agents in nearby Parry Sound.

While two publications from 1985 and 1993 attempt to chronicle Pegahmagabow's astounding war record, both gloss over the struggle against the Canadian government that occupied most of his postwar years. The book *Forgotten Soldiers*, by Canadian War

Museum historian Fred Gaffen, and the Veterans Affairs publication *Native Soldiers, Foreign Battlefields* tell only the story of the young, idealistic soldier and nothing of the bitter veteran who was dismissed as mentally unbalanced by both Indian Affairs and the Department of Soldiers' Civil Re-establishment (now Veterans Affairs Canada).[4]

Elected chief of the Parry Island band in 1921, Pegahmagabow met and was influenced by Frederick Ogilvie Loft, a Six Nations Mohawk who had served as a lieutenant in France with the Canadian Overseas Railway Construction Corps and in Britain with the Canadian Forestry Corps. During the 1920s, Loft founded and served as president of the League of Indians of Canada, the predecessor to all the national native political organizations that exist today.

As the years passed, Pegahmagabow became increasingly outspoken on the issue of native rights. In October 1943, he was a member of a national delegation that demonstrated on Parliament Hill in Ottawa for the exemption of natives from income tax and conscription. He later became a member of the National Indian Government after it was formed in Ottawa in June 1945, and served two terms as supreme chief.

As Peter Kulchyski pointed out in an article on Frederick Loft in the *Native Studies Review*, it is a commonplace assumption today that native political activism began or "emerged" in the early 1960s with the American civil rights movement, the extension of the franchise, the federal government's community development program of the early 1960s, and so on.[5] That such a resurgence of native activism occurred in this period is beyond question, he wrote. But the problem with these assumptions is they both ignore the intense struggles carried on by native people prior to the 1960s and tend to imply that non-native forces were responsible for the birth of native activism.

Francis Pegahmagabow was an early leader in the fight for

native self-government, fuelled by his feelings of abandonment by the Canadian government in the postwar years. In many ways a man ahead of his time, he helped set out the course followed by Canada's native leaders.

In 1967, fifteen years after his death, Pegahmagabow was one of twenty-seven natives honoured by inclusion in the Indian Hall of Fame, on display in the museum in the Woodland Indian Cultural Educational Centre in Brantford, Ontario.[6] The Hall of Fame recognizes Indians who in some field of endeavour excelled and contributed substantially to the situation of Canada's aboriginal peoples. Pegahmagabow stands in the distinguished company of Joseph Brant, Tecumseh, Louis Riel, Poundmaker, and Thunderchild. Others in the Hall of Fame include internationally acclaimed poet Pauline Johnson; legendary long-distance runners Tom Longboat and Joseph Benjamin Keeper; Toronto Maple Leafs captain George Armstrong; Brigadier-General Oliver Milton Martin, the first native appointed to a judicial post in Ontario; and Alberta Lieutenant-Governor Ralph Steinhauer, the first native appointed to the position in any province.

During the 1920s, Pegahmagabow sought the equality and respect that he had enjoyed while in the trenches by joining the 23rd Northern Pioneers, a militia regiment with its headquarters in Parry Sound. He was the sergeant-major of "A" Company from the spring of 1930 until December 1936, when the regiment was absorbed into the existing Algonquin Regiment and his involvement ended.

The Algonquin Regiment was mobilized for active service on July 22, 1940. Several of the young men Pegahmagabow trained during summer camps at New Liskeard, Orillia, Huntsville, Owen Sound, and Penetanguishene went into combat with the regiment during the Second World War. One of them, Percy Ball, questioned in a 1989 interview why there wasn't a plaque in Parry Sound honouring the decorated warrior.[7] He revered Pegahmagabow as the most honourable man he'd ever met.

At the unveiling of a plaque honouring members of the Algonquin Regiment, in particular Francis Pegahmagabow, the many representatives of the Pegahmagabow family included the veteran's two surviving children, Duncan Pegahmagabow and Marie Anderson.

On July 26, 2003, local veterans of the regiment unveiled a plaque that explains the origins of the Rotary and Algonquin Regiment Fitness Trail and honours those who were a part of the Algonquin Regiment, in particular Francis Pegahmagabow. Royal Canadian Legion Branch 117 in Parry Sound instituted the Francis Pegahmagabow Memorial Bursary, worth up to $1,000 for a financially needy child or grandchild of a veteran or ex-Canadian military personnel graduating from Parry Sound High School to pursue college, university, or an accredited apprenticeship program.

A short time after the unveiling of the plaque in Parry Sound, Pegahmagabow's youngest child, Marie Anderson, travelled to Ottawa with about three dozen relatives to present officials at the Canadian War Museum with his military decorations and medals, the headdress he wore as an Ojibwa chief, and several other artifacts associated with his life. "When this was brought to our attention, that the family was interested in donating his medals, it was very exciting for us," said Tim Cook, the museum's First World War historian. "He's a very significant figure from the war."[8] Unfortunately, a vintage rifle the family believed might be the actual weapon Pegahmagabow carried during the war was identified by the museum's collections manager for arms and armour as a Winchester model dating from 1924.[9]

When the new Canadian War Museum opened on LeBreton Flats in May 2005, the Pegahmagabow family and other visitors at last learned exactly how "significant" Pegahmagabow had been. In "The Hundred Days" pod in the First World War gallery, the text accompanying a permanent stand-alone display of his medals and headdress officially identifies him as "the most decorated First Peoples soldier in Canadian military history." He is displayed alongside the Canadian Corps commander, General Sir Arthur Currie, and two Victoria Cross (VC) winners—Sergeant Thomas Ricketts and Lieutenant Samuel Lewis Honey. A Newfoundlander, Ricketts was awarded his VC for braving heavy machine-gun fire and helping to outflank a German battery a month before the war ended, becoming the youngest recipient in the British army. Honey won his VC two weeks earlier for single-handedly capturing a German machine-gun nest and ten prisoners.

During the summer of 2006 the Canadian Armed Forces finally gave Pegahmagabow long-overdue recognition by officially naming a building after him at Canadian Forces Base Borden. The colourful ceremony, attended by Ontario Lieutenant-Governor James Bartleman, himself a member of Rama First Nation, christened the 3rd Canadian Ranger Patrol Group's headquarters as the Corporal Francis Pegahmagabow, MM, Building. Organizers seamlessly combined military pomp and speeches with Midewiwin spiritualism, drummers, and smudging in an event that also included the unveiling of a portrait and cairn, traditional native foods, and a display of Pegahmagabow's medals and headdress from the Canadian War Museum.

"Today, is not about opening a building. It is not about bricks and mortar. It is about recognizing an outstanding individual, a warrior and a war hero who placed service before self," Brigadier General G.R. Thibault, commander of Land Force Central Area, told the crowd. "Decorated three times for his actions during the Great War, Francis Pegahmagabow embodies the characteristics I wish to instil in my Rangers and offer to my junior ones as a role model: Resilience, Fortitude, Discipline, Decisiveness and Courage. Francis Pegahmagabow, a volunteer soldier, stands out as a professional. His actions, of the highest order, provide a sterling example of how adversity brings out the best in people."[10]

The process to name the 3rd Canadian Ranger Patrol Group headquarters building at CFB Borden after Pegahmagabow began in June 2005, shortly after the commanding officer, Major Keith Lawrence, and public affairs ranger Sergeant Peter Moon, happened upon the permanent Pegahmagabow exhibit at the war museum. Both had heard of the exploits of Thomas George Prince, Military Medal and U.S. Silver Star, a Manitoba aboriginal veteran of the Second World War and Korean War who died in 1977—there's a street and a park in Winnipeg named after Sergeant Prince, as well as a barracks at CFB Petawawa, and a monument honours him as "Canada's most decorated aboriginal war veteran."[11] Neither, however, had heard of Pegahmagabow.

"Peter Moon and I looked at each other and it just flashed," Major Lawrence explained in an interview months before the June 6, 2006, ceremony. "This is it. And the realization that it wasn't Sergeant Prince who was the most decorated. This was the guy and he was being highlighted as an aboriginal soldier. I just thought that brought everything together ... By naming our building after him, it's the first stage in righting a perceived wrong or misconception. It allows us to get [Pegahmagabow's] story out a little more."[12]

The Rangers were established in 1947 as a Cold War means to patrol remote northern regions for signs of Soviet intrusions. They number about 4,500 reservists divided into five groups across the country. Often involved in search-and-rescue operations, they also frequently provide help when flooding or forest fires threaten northern communities. In the fall of 2005, the 3rd Canadian Ranger Patrol Group—composed almost entirely of 400 Cree, Oji-Cree, and Ojibwa reservists living in isolated northern Ontario communities—assisted with the evacuation of Kashechewan during the tainted water crisis.

According to Major Lawrence, the protocol to name a building after a person requires approval throughout the military chain of command right up to the Directorate of History at National Defence Headquarters. "In our cases, we have a lot to do with First Nations, so naming it after this individual meets the criterion of appropriateness. It's a defined process that usually takes about six months," he said. "This one just sailed through with no objections whatsoever."[13]

Although Anishinabek Nation Grand Council Chief John Beaucage said it was exciting that Pegahmagabow was being acknowledged, he also expressed regret that only the youngest of the veteran's eight children, Marie Anderson, is still alive. "I think it's a wonderful thing that there's this recognition. All too often the native veterans have been the ones left out in the cold," he said. "It's unfortunate that it comes after Francis's death and it comes after the death of Francis's son Duncan [who died in November 2004]. It would have been wonderful if all of the family could have been involved with seeing the recognition of Francis."[14]

Marie Anderson told Aboriginal Peoples Television Network reporter Donna Smith that her strongest memories of her father were of his teaching her how to spear fish and her falling into the icy water. "This is something I never, ever expected to see," she said. "I'm really proud of the way he's getting his recognition, even though it's been quite a while since he died."[15]

Perhaps the greatest recognition that could be bestowed upon Francis Pegahmagabow is still to come. In the spring of 2005, Wasauksing First Nation and Parks Canada co-operated on a submission to the Historic Sites and Monuments Board of Canada (HSMBC) to have Pegahmagabow recognized as a Canadian of national historic importance. Apparently, there has been no formal decision yet. The written submission, which recommends a plaque on Wasauksing First Nation, offers the following summary of significance:

> *Pegahmagabow is recognized by the Canadian War Museum as the most decorated aboriginal soldier in Canadian history.*
>
> *During his political leadership after the First World War, he used his notoriety as a war hero to his advantage in fighting for self-determination and against restrictions placed upon First Nations by the Department of Indian Affairs.*
>
> *He was chief of his band, a delegate to national aboriginal assemblies and supreme chief of the National Indian Government.*[16]

While HSMBC has recognized thirteen aboriginals for military endeavours, only two survived into the twentieth century. Most were nineteenth-century figures such as Métis leaders Louis Riel and Gabriel Dumont, recognized for the Northwest Rebellion, Plains Cree chief Poundmaker, and Shawnee leader Tecumseh.

Only eight First World War veterans have been commemorated. These include VC-winning aces Lieutenant-Colonel William Avery Bishop and Lieutenant-Colonel William George Barker, Canadian Corps commander General Sir Arthur Currie, "In Flanders Fields" author Lieutenant-Colonel John McCrae, and Lieutenant Wilfred Reid May, one of Canada's leading bush pilots of the postwar era. The list includes Tom Longboat, the long-distance runner from Six Nations Grand River Reserve who served overseas as a despatch runner but who was recognized for his sports achievements such as winning the 1907 Boston Marathon.

The only other person previously submitted to HSMBC whose life mirrors Pegahmagabow was Sergeant Prince, who became one of the leading Indian rights advocates in Manitoba during the late 1940s. While the board recognized Prince's life had been both brave and tragic, it was not prepared to recommend that he was an individual of historic significance at the national level.

Unfortunately, recognition and notoriety can have unforeseen ramifications, such as in 2007, when the federal Conservative government tossed Pegahmagabow's name into an explanation for why the minister of Indian and Northern Affairs, Jim Prentice, was absent from the Assembly of First Nations annual general assembly in Halifax. This was just days after the Conservatives had announced that their government wasn't obligated to financially support the wide-ranging Kelowna Accord, signed by the former Liberal government of Paul Martin in November 2005, which would have seen $5 billion go toward First Nations education, employment, and anti-poverty initiatives. In a July 12, 2007, speech to the assembly, parliamentary secretary Rod Bruinooge explained that Prentice was in Belgium attending ceremonies marking the 90th anniversary of the Battle of Passchendaele, where his great-uncle had fought.

Aboriginal leaders grumbled that Prentice should have been there to explain the government's position on the Kelowna Accord. "We think we were snubbed by him not making time to come here," Rick Simon, an Atlantic regional chief with the assembly, told the Canadian Press. "It shows where the priority is, and we're not."[17]

However, in his speech and in a press release, Bruinooge stated that Prentice was also in Belgium to honour Corporal Francis Pegahmagabow, Canada's most-decorated aboriginal soldier, who had fought at Passchendaele. Then, using a line lifted from the Veterans Affairs publication *Native Soldiers, Foreign Battlefields*, he remarked, "I am told that the corporal's son, Duncan Pegahmagabow, remembers that his father was always saying we have to live in harmony with all living things in the world. When the minister asked me to attend this year's annual general assembly he urged me to carry on Corporal Pegahmagabow's message of respect and collaboration to the Assembly of First Nations and its executive and member communities, so that we can work together harmoniously."[18]

Clearly, Indian and Northern Affairs would rather forget that Pegahmagabow had, in fact, spent his entire postwar life actively defying the Indian agents and fighting the government's policies concerning aboriginals.

The original headstone erected by Veterans Affairs Canada did not recognize that Cpl. Francis Pegahmagabow had won the Military Medal a total of three times. Minister of Veterans Affairs Fred J. Mifflin acknowledged the error in correspondence with the author and a new stone was placed in the cemetery at Wasauksing First Nation in October 1997.

CHAPTER I

The Young Man

THE WORLD into which Francis Pegahmagabow was born more than a century ago was quite different from that in which white Canadians of the same period lived. The Indian Act of 1876 and its subsequent revisions made Indians wards of the federal government, to be treated as minors without the full privileges of citizenship, although its primary goal was to encourage assimilation into Canadian society and economic self-sufficiency. Indians were not even permitted to vote in Canadian federal elections until 1960.

The Indian Act placed all Indian reserve lands in the trust of the Crown and stated that this land could not be mortgaged or seized for defaulted debts, nor could it be taxed. All land sales, and sales of timber and mineral resources, had to be approved by the majority of adult male band members and the superintendent-general of Indian Affairs. Ignoring the aboriginal system of hereditary chiefs, the Act also imposed the concept of elected chiefs and councils.

The legislation was administered in the native communities by local Indian agents, or superintendents, who had tremendous power in that band council decisions were invalid unless they were present at the meeting and approved. Peter S. Schmalz, in *The Ojibwa of Southern Ontario*, quotes past-president of the National

FACING PAGE Francis Pegahmagabow, 1912. *(Duncan Pegahmagabow)*

Indian Brotherhood George Manuel: "It was the job of these new white chiefs to displace our traditional leaders in their care over our day-to-day lives in order to bring our way of life into line with the policies that had been decreed in Ottawa."[1] The agent acted as a judge in civil disputes, accepted bids and oversaw all construction on the reserve, purchased all supplies, including livestock, seed, and implements, and sold all farm produce.

Francis Pegahmagabow was most likely born March 9, 1889, on the reserve known today as Shawanaga First Nation, just north of Parry Sound, although he told military authorities in 1914 that he was born two years later.[2] The son of Michael Pegahmagabow of the Parry Island band and Mary Contin of the Henvey Inlet band, located farther north up the Georgian Bay shore, Francis became the subject of intense scrutiny by Indian Affairs early in his life, after the death of his father in the spring of 1891.

When Dr. Thomas Smith Walton, the Indian superintendent at Parry Sound, travelled north to Shawanaga in April 1891 to pay the annual Robinson Huron Treaty annuities to band members, he learned of Michael Pegahmagabow's death earlier that month. He also discovered that Michael's wife had returned to her own band, leaving her child, whom Walton guessed to be three years old, in the care of her husband's maternal uncle Peter Pamagewong.[3]

The young child became the subject of numerous letters back and forth between Indian Affairs and Dr. Walton, who wondered if Pamagewong should be appointed legal guardian and, consequently, to whom he should pay Michael Pegahmagabow's treaty money.

By October, the Shawanaga band council had entrusted the care of Francis Pegahmagabow to Noah Nebimanyquod, an elderly band member who had raised Michael Pegahmagabow following the deaths of both of his parents many years before. The band argued that while Pamagewong may have been the child's uncle, Nebimanyquod was his adopted grandfather.[4]

Chief James Pegahmagabow Jr. of the Parry Island band, Fran-

Parry Sound Indian agent Dr. Thomas Smith Walton (right) with sons
Fred (left) and Ernest. Appointed in April 1884, Dr. Walton held the
position until dismissed in June 1897 after an investigation into allegations
that he had profited personally from the sale of timber on the Shawanaga
reserve. More likely, Walton, who had campaigned feverishly for Conservative candidate George McCormick in the Parry Sound-Muskoka
constituency prior to the June 1896 election, felt the repercussions of
his partisanship when voters ended the 18-year reign of Prime Minister
John A. Macdonald and the Conservatives, in favour of Wilfrid Laurier's
Liberals. (*John Macfie*)

cis's great uncle, told Dr. Walton he approved of the child being raised by Nebimanyquod at Shawanaga, where he fit in better socially than on Parry Island, although he remained a Parry Island band member through his father's lineage. As it turned out, Chief Pegahmagabow himself died from consumption within the next three years, leaving his widow, Mary, destitute and with several children of her own to care for.[5]

"With the Indian people the family is very important, the extended family," explained Duncan Pegahmagabow in a 1990 interview, when he was 53. "Supposing a child was left without parents, it was not a total loss. The child was never left without somebody. That's the way my father grew up as he was an orphan. He went from family to family."[6] However, both Duncan and his sister Marie Anderson, 64 when interviewed in 2005, believed that their father lived most of his childhood with the family of Frank Kewaquedo. "He said he doesn't complain about the way he was raised, but he said he really struggled to fit in," said Marie. "Indian Affairs, I guess, give him a bit of a clothing allowance and stuff. It would go to another young boy in that family."[7]

While growing up at Shawanaga, Pegahmagabow was steeped in the customs, traditions, and rituals of the Ojibwa, and a recent article examines what he told Canadian government anthropologist Diamond Jenness in 1929, and what his narratives reveal about him as an individual. According to the authors, it was standard at the time for ethnographers to submerge the personalities and proclivities of their informants to sell the idea of a consensus invisibly imposed on the culture, at the cost of the contesting opinions of informants that do not neatly fit into the cultural norms they imposed. The authors assert that Jenness in his work exhibited a distinct tendency to allow for the individual voice of his informants to ring loud and clear.[8]

It emerges from the Jenness ethnology *The Ojibwa Indians of Parry Island: Their Social and Religious Life*, published in 1935, that a

TOP Lower Indian village on Parry Island, October 1910. (*H.J. Woodside /
Library and Archives Canada, PA-16814*)

BOTTOM Indian burial ground at lower Indian village, Parry Island, circa
1890. (*Frank W. Micklethwaite / Library and Archives Canada, PA-68316*)

woman Pegahmagabow refers to as his "foster mother" practised traditional medicine: "When I was living with my foster-parents at Shawanaga one of their daughters reached maturity. My foster-mother put wild ginger in all our food to prevent any ill-effect and she gave me wild ginger to chew."[9]

It was probably under the influence of his foster mother that Pegahmagabow gained the strong traditional sense of medicine that he carried into adulthood and on to the battlefields of the First World War. Authors John Steckley and Bryan Cummins give the following illustrative examples:

Talk to the tree or plant when you are gathering its bark, leaves, or root. Tell its soul and shadow why you are taking away part of its body. Say to it "Help me to cure such and such a malady." Unless you do this your medicine will not be of much avail. Moreover, if it is the root of the plant you need, take only part of it and leave the stem if possible undisturbed.[10]

Pegahmagabow's deer medicine is the root of the shingoak-wansiwan *("pine-shaped herb," probably the mugwort, Artemisia dracunoloides). He must find the plant to his right, for if it lies to his left it has no virtue. He buries the stem in the ground with a little tobacco, chews the root, and rubs the mingled juice and saliva over his eyes. Then he can approach a deer close enough to kill it with a tomahawk.*[11]

Pegahmagabow had a powerful sense of surviving through spiritual protection, which probably originated with the fact that in 1891 he lived through the severe illness that killed his father and sickened his mother. Marie Anderson, in fact, spoke of a Shawanaga neighbour who, suspecting something was wrong, paddled from the mainland over to Snake Island to check on the family and found Francis near death.[12] In what was perhaps a separate incident, Pegahmagabow told Jenness about being poisoned by a hognose snake when he was a baby, but a *kusabindugeyu* discovered the cause of his illness and cured him.[13]

More powerful and threatening is the following story later in his life at Shawanaga:

> *When I was a young man at Shawanaga a* medewadji *tried several nights in succession to carry away my soul. I am sure it was a conjuror who was trying to harm me, because my father and grandfather had offended some of the Indians on Lake Huron, and these Indians destroyed by sorcery every member of their families except myself.*[14]

Steckley and Cummins wrote that the fact that Pegahmagabow repeatedly survived battles in which many of his fellow soldiers were killed or wounded and became one of the few Canadian soldiers who experienced virtually the entire war, may have led him to a belief that he was protected while others were not. Conversely, they wrote, being raised with a sense of spiritual protection and rescue could possibly have enabled him to engage in trench warfare without fear and with a feeling that he was in some way protected.[15]

Childhood dreams held a special importance for the Ojibwa and for Pegahmagabow. Every dream, however insignificant it might appear, carried a meaning or warning, he told Jenness. Dreams inspired some men to become great warriors, others to gain power and influence as medicine-men.

In his Parry Island ethnography, Jenness wrote:

> *Every morning, even now, Pegahmagabow lies beside his two boys, seven and nine years old, respectively, and asks them what dreams have come to them during the night. When he himself was about seven years of age his foster-parents made him swallow a little gunpowder so that his soul and shadow might become more alert*

and observant, and, therefore, more prepared for a visit and bless-ing from some manido a few years later. For the same purpose other lads had to swallow a mixture of charcoal and some other substances."[16]

Almost a half-century after his childhood, Pegahmagabow re-called a powerful vision in a brief biographical sketch, perhaps penned in response to a 1951 letter from Lethbridge, Alberta, MP John Blackmore, an honorary Blackfoot chief, who wanted to know more about him and how he had become supreme chief of the National Indian Government.[17]

Pegahmagabow wrote:

A native orphan boy at Shawanaga ... had often gone to pray and cry by the graves of his dead parents. One time, he fell asleep there. At the dawn the next morning someone said to him, "Awake my boy, do not cry anymore, you are now a great person. You have been blessed to save your tribes from slavery." He kept that to himself. Then another day came an age-old native [who] was about to die. The foster mother was informed by the old age to take good care of the same orphan boy. "He has a very special, wonderful blessing. He will save our tribes from slavery when he get to be a man."[18]

From the age of seven, Jenness wrote, Ojibwa boys were taught the skills needed to hunt and fish. Neighbours, especially men, were invited to share the feast when a boy killed his first game, so that they might invoke the blessing of the Great Spirit on the household and encourage the lad to further efforts.[19]

To harden their bodies, boys were encouraged to wrestle and run races, Jenness wrote, and every child, boy or girl, had to bathe in a lake or river at the beginning of each month until freeze-up. In winter they ran naked to a mark on the ice, or were driven out into a snowstorm and rubbed with snow.[20]

Duncan Pegahmagabow recalled being told by Shawanaga elder

Parry Island musicians, 1912. Front (left to right): Jonas Nanibush, Adam L. King (bandmaster), Henry Jackson, Elijah Tronche, Alec S. King, Francis Pegahmagabow. Rear (left to right): Henry Hawke, Willie W. King, Lewis Lamondiere, David W. King, Tom Trembles. *(David L. Thomas Collection / Archives of Ontario, C 253, Tray 11-13)*

Solomon Pawis that Francis had not been very healthy during his early childhood, but he was determined to build his body up by running back and forth every day between the village and the shoreline. "In other words, his health came back," Duncan said. "He became a healthy young man."[21]

Department of Marine and Fisheries lighthouse tenders *Simcoe* and *Lambton* moored at the Parry Sound base. The *Lambton*, on which Francis Pegahmagabow served as a seaman before the First World War, went down in Lake Superior with her crew of 22 on April 19, 1922. The *Simcoe* foundered with all hands in the Gulf of St. Lawrence on December 7, 1917.
(Author's collection)

Little else is known about Francis Pegahmagabow's childhood at Shawanaga other than it must have been a very hard existence. Although his mother returned to Shawanaga and married Joseph Giskibus in 1892, it's significant that Pegahmagabow always referred to himself as an orphan and even told the military that he had no family.[22] By the age of 12 he was employed in the local lumber camps. He later worked for George Stalker, who operated a fishing station on the Mink Islands, as well as another fisherman, William Henry Oldfield, based on Double Island, near the Point au Baril lighthouse.[23] He then turned up on Parry Island in time for the 1911 census, at which time he gave his age as 21.

Despite his advanced age, Pegahmagabow had a strong desire to complete his public school education. He approached the Parry Island band council several times in the fall of 1911 to have the band pay for his room and board in nearby Parry Sound while he attended classes. Towards the end of the year, he paid numerous visits to Parry Sound Crown attorney Walter Lockwood Haight asking him to intercede on his behalf. Impressed with Pegahmagabow's strong desire to better himself, Haight wrote Chief Peter Megis a letter threatening to take the matter up with Indian Affairs if the band denied an education to such a "bright, promising boy who ought to be encouraged in every way."[24]

Seamen aboard the *Simcoe* retrieve a Georgian Bay navigation buoy. This is the type of work Francis Pegahmagabow would have performed for the Department of Marine and Fisheries. (*Author's collection*)

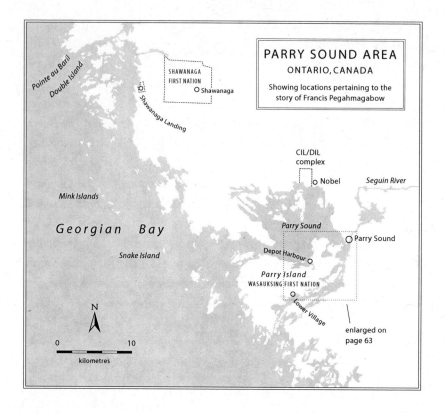

In January 1912, the Parry Island council passed a resolution to pay Pegahmagabow's board while he attended school in Parry Sound for five months. Indian agent Duncan Fraser Macdonald recorded in his personal diary that "Frank Pagamahmagabo [sic] came in and told me he was told by his teacher that he was doing well."[25] It's also apparent that Pegahmagabow was learning to read music, and he performed locally with a group of Parry Island musicians.

"I have a great admiration for the man because he seemed to do a lot of these things on his own," Duncan Pegahmagabow said. "He didn't have the kind of support that, for instance, I would be looking for if I embarked on a musical career, or a career in sports.

I would always tend to look back. But he seemed to thrive on his own determination."[26]

By the summer of 1912, Pegahmagabow's desire to know more about the Great Lakes and the world around him led him to sign up as a seaman on the *Lambton*, a 323-ton Department of Marine and Fisheries ship that sailed Lake Huron and Georgian Bay from the Parry Sound base, tending buoys and delivering supplies to isolated lighthouse keepers. It was during this time, he told Jenness, that he began to write down in notebooks the customs and traditions of other Ojibwa bands with which he came into contact.

A brush with typhoid fever in the spring of 1913, during which Pegahmagabow was nursed back to health by the Sisters of St. Joseph in Parry Sound, seems to have fostered his life-long commitment to Roman Catholicism, even though he continued to believe very strongly in traditional Ojibwa customs and rituals.[27] The following summer, he not only gave $10 to St. Joseph's Hospital, but also made another donation to the poor box at St. Anthony's church.

In thanking Pegahmagabow for his generous donations, Father Gaston Artus, S.J., wrote:

> *I am glad you are going so well. Profit by your opportunities. After a while you will take your papers as an engineer and then you will have a fine position ... Be faithful to your religious duties. Go to mass and receive Holy Communion as often as you can.*[28]

Like Walter Haight, Father Artus was convinced that Pegahmagabow had a bright future.

26

CHAPTER 2

The Warrior

EVENTS THOUSANDS OF MILES away in Sarajevo, Bosnia, di-
verted the probable course of Francis Pegahmagabow's career as
a Department of Marine and Fisheries sailor when the visiting
heir to the Austro-Hungarian throne was assassinated in June
1914, causing Austria, backed by its German allies, to declare war
against Serbia. By July 30, Serbian-allied Russia began mobilizing
its forces and refused a German ultimatum to stop, resulting in
a German declaration of war not only against Russia, but also her
allies, France and Italy.

Pegahmagabow was back at Parry Sound by late summer when
neutral Britain and her colonies, including Canada, declared war
on Germany. The call to arms went out immediately and Canada's
militia regiments began a feverish recruiting spree. In Parry Sound,
the headquarters of the 23rd Northern Pioneers quickly erected a

FACING PAGE Corporal Francis Pegahmagabow, wearing the Military
Medal and Two Bars (left), 1914–1915 Star, British War Medal (1914–1918)
and Allied Victory Medal (1914–1920). He is also wearing the Indian
Treaty Medal presented to Parry Island Chief James Pegahmagabow Sr.
by the Prince of Wales (later King Edward VII) on his visit to Canada in
1860. Richard K. Malott, chief curator of collections (now retired) at the
Canadian War Museum, wrote to the author: "This is a rare photograph
as I have never seen a Canadian Indian soldier wearing his uniform, service medals and an Indian Treaty Medal." (Duncan Pegahmagabow)

tent camp at the local agricultural fairgrounds as a rallying point for volunteers from the regiment's six companies.

One can only speculate what was going through the young Ojibwa's mind when he rushed to the fairgrounds and enlisted in the Northern Pioneers on August 13, within days of the declaration of war. For Pegahmagabow, the hostilities probably presented an opportunity to leave a painful childhood behind and distinguish himself as a warrior in the tradition of his forefathers. So strong was this determination that he wrote to Indian Affairs

Volunteers of the 23rd Northern Pioneers, August 1914.
(Mrs. Doug Sproat)

Of the 23rd Northern Pioneers' entire pre-war complement of officers, only three sailed for England as members of the 1st Canadian Battalion, including Capt. William J. Lalor, who accepted a demotion in rank to lieutenant. By the end of 1918, Lt.-Col. Lalor commanded the 2nd Battalion, Canadian Machine Gun Corps. *(Mrs. Doug Sproat)*

after being wounded in the fall of 1916, pleading to get back into combat so that he could earn more medals.

It's peculiar that a member of the Caribou clan would be so driven to engage in warfare, especially when there was no compelling defensive reason and his participation was not expected by his peers, his family, or the Canadian government. Traditionally, people of Caribou, Deer, or Hoof clans were said to be gentle like the deer, moose, or caribou for whom they were named. They were pacifists and would not use harsh words of any kind. They were the poets of the Ojibwa.[1] Although it's clear from his discussions with anthropologist Diamond Jenness that clan membership held a special significance for Pegahmagabow, he had in fact spent most of his childhood with non-Caribou clan families.[2]

In a rare 1919 interview with a *Toronto Evening Telegram* reporter, Pegahmagabow said that he would immediately go to war again if asked, even though he was a treaty Indian and thus had no obligation to do so. He stated bluntly, "I went to war voluntarily just as quick as the white man."[3]

It is a fact that many natives and non-whites volunteered to fight in the war, with the hope that assuming equal responsibilities would earn them equal opportunities in Canadian society. In an article on the enlistment of visible minorities in the Canadian Expeditionary Force, James W. St. G. Walker wrote that in many instances the struggle became a community effort: communities encouraged, organized, and financed the enlistment of their young men, and those men volunteered in order to gain recognition and to further the rights of the whole community.[4] However, in this case, Pegahmagabow seems to have acted of his own resolve.

At the start of the war, native enlistments went relatively unnoticed by the Canadian military, which did not record racial origins on attestation forms, and also by Indian Affairs, which did not attempt to keep records on Indians who had volunteered. Not until November 1915 did Duncan Campbell Scott, the deputy superintendent of Indian Affairs, instruct Indian agents to send him information on all Indian soldiers from their agencies. In February 1917, Scott provided agents with a departmental form on which to update their original lists. In addition, agents were instructed to include any pertinent information concerning an Indian's war record, decorations, and background.

Pegahmagabow's early enlistment is unusual. Of the 400 aboriginal First World War soldiers from western Canada studied by L. James Dempsey in his book *Warriors of the King*, for example, only three enlisted in 1914.[5] However, it is believed that by the end of the war between 3,500 and 4,000 Indians had enlisted out of a possible total of 11,500 eligible for service. This was approaching thirty-five per cent enlistment and was at least equal to the rate in the white population of Canada.[6]

Ironically, while the Canadian government came to encourage native enlistment after the bloody battles of the Somme in 1916, for well over a year after the outbreak of the war the supply of volunteers exceeded the demand and recruiting officers could afford to be extremely selective. Within days of the first shots in Europe, the Militia Council forbade the enlistment of Indians. Even as late as October 1915 the Surgeon General advised Indian Affairs:

> *I would point out that it has been decided that while British troops would be proud to be associated with their Indian fellow subjects, the Germans might refuse to extend to them the privileges of civilized warfare* ...[7]

As the volunteers of the Northern Pioneers marched around the Parry Sound countryside and practised countless hours of musketry, the minister of Militia and Defence, Colonel Sam Hughes, scrapped Canada's entire mobilization plan and decided instead to raise new battalions which were to be known by number and thus did not perpetuate the traditional names of the militia regiments. Out on a ten-mile hike to the rifle ranges, the Northern Pioneers unexpectedly received orders on August 20 to board a Canadian Pacific Railway train at Parry Sound and head for Valcartier, outside Quebec City, where no camp yet existed.

At the new camp, the Parry Sound contingent was amalgamated with several hundred other volunteers from Windsor, London, Sarnia, Stratford, and Galt to form the 1st Battalion, otherwise known as the Western Ontario Regiment. While hundreds of officers and recruits were sent home from Valcartier as surplus and not required for the first contingent, Pegahmagabow was judged physically fit for overseas service and swore an oath to King George v on September 15, 1914.[8]

Appointed commander of the 1st Battalion was 48-year-old Frederic William Hill, a lawyer and former mayor of Niagara Falls, Ontario, and until then a major in the 44th Lincoln and Welland Regiment.[9] Pegahmagabow stood before the new commander on September 22 and was accepted by him for service in the battalion.

It is impossible to judge whether Lieutenant-Colonel Hill was aware of the directive forbidding the enlistment of natives or if he simply chose to ignore it, seeing before him only someone whom he felt would make a fine soldier. Obviously, from surviving correspondence carried on between the two men decades after the hostilities ceased, Lieutenant-Colonel Hill came to both respect and revere Pegahmagabow for his battlefield exploits.

As Lieutenant-Colonel Hill was certain Pegahmagabow would

The 1st Canadian Infantry Battalion in parade at Camp Valcartier, 1914.
(Library and Archives Canada, PA-66879)

Brig.-Gen. Frederic W. Hill, DSO, commander of the 9th Canadian Infantry Brigade, July 1918. As a lieutenant-colonel, Hill commanded the 1st Canadian Infantry Battalion from Sept. 1914 to Dec. 1915. *(Library and Archives Canada, PA-2980)*

become a fine soldier, so too was William Ireland, editor of the *Parry Sound North Star* and a major in the Northern Pioneers. At 61 he was far too old for combat in France, although he openly yearned for the opportunity. Ireland wrote of Pegahmagabow's enlistment at some length:

> *His grandfather was a warrior and chief and fought for the British in 1812, so the boy comes by his fighting instincts from a long line of fighting ancestors who fought in the Indian wars. We are all hoping Francis will distinguish himself as his forefathers did and will return home covered with glory and medals. His example might well be followed.*[10]

While many native soldiers, especially those from isolated areas, found the discipline and order of military life to be a huge culture shock, Pegahmagabow seems to have had little problem assimilating into the predominantly white battalion, no doubt due to his previous experience as a crewman aboard the *Lambton*. John Macfie, whose father, Roy, was among the 1st Battalion recruits from the Parry Sound area, wrote that the ever-smiling "Peggy" amused his white colleagues at Valcartier by painting his wigwam-shaped bell tent with traditional Ojibwa symbols. Later, among English civilians, he developed a penchant for passing himself off as a tribal chief.[11]

Arriving in England in September 1914, the Canadians were equipped and drilled on the Salisbury Plain in Wiltshire during the wettest winter in living memory. Apparently, Pegahmagabow corresponded with Parry Sound Indian agent Duncan Fraser Macdonald, who later wrote:

> *I had a letter from Francis Pegamaga [sic] at Salisbury Camp. He is getting tired waiting for to get away to try his hand at shooting. He may thank his stars that he is where he is at present. Well, it's rough and will be rougher before it is quieted down.*[12]

Although it is evident that Pegahmagabow had an extremely limited command of the English language, he did not shy away from letters. He always graciously acknowledged packages sent to him by a group of ladies from Claremont, Ontario, who supplied socks and other comforts to men who had enlisted from the Uxbridge area.[13] They had been given his name by men in his battalion who noticed that he did not receive much mail from home.

The 1st Battalion finally sailed from Avonsmouth on February 8, 1915, aboard the *Architect*, and arrived at St. Nazaire, France, three days later. A freight train carried the men from the coast towards the trenches for a week's indoctrination with the British units holding the line in front of Armentieres. The battalion's four companies were assigned to the 1st Leicestershire Regiment, the 1st Shropshire Regiment, and the 2nd York and Lancashire Regiment.[14]

By the time the Canadians arrived in Europe, the quick advances of the war's early months had bogged down. A continuous front extended between the opposing armies from the North Sea to neutral Switzerland.

It was a relatively quiet sector, but the Canadians were entirely unprepared for what they encountered. The trenches were dug to water level and capped with sandbags. Duckboards on the trench floor covered the foul-smelling water that filtered in. All day long, enemy snipers fired bullets that zinged into the fortifications. Occasionally, shells would scream overhead, accompanied by shouted warnings from the experienced British regulars. At night, German flares soared up into the sky and sank back to the earth, illuminating the landscape in eerie shadows.

During the initial weeks at the front, the troops of the 1st Battalion fell into the routine of holding a section of the trench for several weeks and then moving back behind the lines for baths, a change of clothes, and a brief period of relaxation. Each brief respite was invariably followed by a forced march to relieve another unit somewhere down the line.

By early April 1915, the entire 1st Canadian Division had marched into the Ypres salient, the last Belgian ground still in Allied hands, and it was here that they received their baptism of fire in battle when, on the warm spring evening of April 22, the Germans released the contents of close to 6,000 cylinders of chlorine gas. Borne on a light breeze, the gas rolled in a writhing wall of olive-green vapour over the parapets. Without protection, men either choked and died or—nauseated and sick—broke and fled, leaving a four-mile-wide hole in the Allied defences. This first use of gas, a direct violation of the Hague Convention governing the conduct of warfare, allowed the enemy to advance some two miles before digging in, awaiting supplies and reinforcements.

Life in the trenches, May 1917. *(Library and Archives Canada, PA-1326)*

That night, Canadian troops worked desperately to close the gap and prevent further advances.

The 1st and 4th Canadian battalions received orders to co-operate with a French counter-attack against the German lines in front of the village of Pilkem early in the morning of April 23, 1915. At 5 a.m., the planned time of the attack, there was still nothing to be seen of the French. But in the early light of dawn, the Canadians could clearly see the Germans on Mauser Ridge, 1,500 yards away, feverishly digging in and laying barbed-wire entanglements. Long, gentle slopes led to the enemy positions atop a ridge that stood barely thirty feet above the surrounding fields.[15]

Just before 5:30 a.m., the 4th Battalion commander, Lieutenant-Colonel Arthur Birchall, gave the order to attack, mistakenly believing he saw the French troops to his left moving forward. With bayonets fixed, the Canadians began to charge.

The Germans held their fire allowing the Canadians to advance closer. When they did fire, it was with devastating impact. Rifle and machine-gun bullets riddled the ranks of the Canadians, and within moments shrapnel shells began to pound the earth. Corporal Edgar Wackett of the 1st Battalion later wrote: "It did not seem possible that any human being should live in the rain of shot and shell that began to play upon us as we advanced...For a time every other man seemed to fall."[16]

In describing the experiences of the Canadians in Flanders in 1915, author Daniel G. Dancocks wrote that shellfire was one of the worst experiences a soldier could have.

The mind-numbing, near-deafening noise and bone-rattling vibrations were bad enough, but the wounds were worse—much worse. At its worst a bursting shell could disintegrate a man, so that nothing recognizable remained of him. Less spectacular, but sometimes as deadly, shell-blast could create over-pressures or vacuums in the body organs, rupturing lungs and producing haemorrhages in the brain and spinal cord.[17]

The majority of injuries came from splinters and shrapnel balls, which could inflict several large or many small wounds on the same person, Dancocks explained. The splinters were irregular in shape, so produced a very rough wound with a great deal of tissue damage, and they frequently carried fragments of clothing or other foreign matter into the body, which made infection almost inevitable.

By 7:30 that morning, the attack had stopped dead some 500 yards from the crest of the ridge and the survivors took cover in the shell holes and in hastily dug trenches on the battlefield. As the Germans continued to bombard them they had little choice but to endure. Anyone attempting to flee would have been hit by enemy snipers and machine-gunners.

Late in the afternoon, the British 13th Brigade launched an attack on the ridge, joined by survivors of the 1st and 4th Canadian Battalions. After an hour and a half of fighting, during which no one came within thirty yards of the ridge, the two Canadian and eight British battalions staggered back and dug in 600 yards from the enemy's position. Later that night, the 1st Battalion moved to the rear, having suffered 400 casualties of all ranks, including fifty-nine dead and thirty-four missing.

Again, it is impossible to know what was going through Pegahmagabow's mind that morning as he saw the carnage all around him, but he clearly believed he was invincible. From conversations he had with Jenness in 1929, it's known that Pegahmagabow had an ardent belief in native customs, visions, and the supernatural. It's not worth debating whether Pegahmagabow did, in fact, lead a charmed life—the fact is that he firmly believed it and took chances accordingly.

"When I was at Rossport, on Lake Superior, in 1914, some of us landed from our vessel to gather blueberries near an Ojibwa camp," he told Jenness. "An old Indian recognized me, and gave me a tiny medicine-bag to protect me, saying I would shortly go into great danger. The bag was of skin, tightly bound with a leather thong. Sometimes it seemed to be hard as a rock, at other times it appeared to contain nothing. What was really inside it I do not know. I wore it in the trenches..."[18]

Another of Pegahmagabow's beliefs was that chewing a dead twig in times of danger offered significant protection. "Well, I couldn't believe it, but I tried it and it sure enough works all right," recalled Levi Nanibush, who was advised to try it during his Second World War service with the Royal Canadian Artillery. "Give you a little bit of encouragement. I was not afraid of anything because of what he told me."[19]

It's not necessary to detail the involvement of the 1st Battalion through the battle of Givenchy in June 1915 and the innumerable raids on the enemy trenches. Pegahmagabow became a survivor—one of the few as the number of originals who had been with the battalion at Valcartier rapidly dwindled. By August 26, Pegahmagabow had received his first stripe, being promoted lance corporal.

It was during the periods of relative inactivity between the fighting that Pegahmagabow came to distinguish himself most. Perhaps drawing on instincts developed while stalking game through the bush, he became a scout—going out alone, mostly at night, to detect and report back on the enemy's movements. Scouting provided ample opportunities to prove his fearlessness. John Macfie commented on this:

> *Most soldiers act like ordinary people. They are scared stiff in the front line, and expose themselves to danger only to the extent that military law demands. But Pegahmagabow went looking for it. He preferred to work alone, in the dark, even infiltrating an enemy trench to stand among its occupants just for the fun of it. He blithely explained to his trench mates that his life was protected by a charm imparted by an old Ojibwa before he left for overseas, so it was no big deal.[20]*

He also became widely known as a sniper, a job that required staying camouflaged and motionless for long periods of time while waiting for a fleeting opportunity to take aim at careless enemy soldiers hundreds of yards away, behind the relative safety of their own lines. It was a task for which men were hand-picked, not only for their sharp eyes and marksmanship, but also for their incredible patience.

As the war progressed and the use and training of snipers became more formalized, schools were established for Canadian marksmen both in England and in France, one of the first being at Bernes-en-Artois in September 1916. Sharpshooters were sent for schooling that included all aspects of sniping and intelligence: map reading and drawing, using aerial photographs, signalling, night movement, information and reports, and patrol formations.[21] However, there is no indication that Pegahmagabow was ever sent on such a training course, although one would expect a four-week absence from the 1st Battalion to be noted in his personnel file, especially since there would have been a formal order authorizing his attendance.

One of Pegahmagabow's Parry Sound contemporaries, Roy Macfie, wrote to the *North Star* in December 1962:

I was interested in reading your remarks about my old pal Francis Pegahmagabow. We enlisted the same day in Parry Sound and served several years together in the same battalion in France. Peggy was a fearless and upright man. He was a wonderful shot and became battalion sniper, although he was only a boy at the time. In my mind I can still see the solid stand of him, and the broad smile...[22]

The fact that Macfie used the term "battalion sniper" is significant because to a infantry soldier of the First World War, this had a special meaning. A battalion sniper was one of twenty-eight men working directly under the battalion intelligence officer to gather information about enemy activity along the battalion's entire frontage, such as artillery activity, trench mortar activity, machine guns and sniping, patrols, movements, and the nature of the enemy's defences, all of which was summarized and sent daily to battalion headquarters. Company snipers, usually less skilled and working in pairs, worked from dusk until dawn from the confines of the section of trench held by their company.[23]

In March 1916, a Royal Warrant instituted the Military Medal as the third-highest gallantry award for noncommissioned officers and soldiers, behind only the coveted Victoria Cross and the Distinguished Conduct Medal. Pegahmagabow was among the first seventy-eight Canadian soldiers recognized with the award in the *London Gazette* of June 3, 1916. Three others from the 1st Battalion were also cited to receive the decoration in the same issue.[24]

In *The Military Medal: Canadian Recipents, 1916–1922*, authors Harry and Cindy Abbink wrote:

> *Recipents of the Military Medal did not capture the public imagination to nearly the same degree as did recipients of the highest gallantry decoration, the Victoria Cross. Unlike VC recipients, schools, bridges and mountain peaks were not named in recognition of their gallant deeds. In fact, unlike the VC and DCM, MM citations were not usually published in the* London Gazette, *and remain obscure as a result. And yet, the deeds that earned them this recognition were not insignificant or inconsequential. Victory was not often solely achieved by the outstanding heroism of VC recipients, but was largely dependent on numerous smaller acts of bravery, often unnoticed and unrecorded. In many of these instances men went one step beyond what duty required, and placing their fear aside, risked death or severe injury to achieve an objective—the cumulative effect of these brief instances of bravery was to spearhead the drive to victory.*[25]

Not all acts of personal courage were rewarded with a medal, as it was common practice to allot a particular number of each award to the various units involved in an engagement. It was left to the commanding officer to determine how the allotted awards should be distributed. In *Vimy*, Pierre Berton records an instance of ten gallant soldiers drawing numbered slips of paper from a helmet to determine who among them would receive the single allotted MM.[26] Frequently, the soldiers themselves did not know what deed of heroism they were rewarded for. Many men first knew of their commendation only when they were called out for a decoration parade and summoned to the fore. Several months may have passed since the event that earned them the award.

Such may have been the case with Pegahmagabow, who apparently told Parry Sound Indian agent Alexander Logan in May 1919 that he had won the MM during the Second Battle of Ypres in 1915.[27] In August 1919, a *Toronto Evening Telegram* reporter, clearly unfamiliar with the battles of the First World War, wrote that Pegahmagabow had earned the MM at Mount Sorrel, a battle which took place June 2–16, 1916.[28]

A recently discovered document indicates that the commanding officer of the 1st Battalion, Lieutenant-Colonel Frank Albert Creighton, originally recommended Pegahmagabow for a Distinguished Conduct Medal on March 1, 1916:

For continuous service as messenger from February 14th 1915 to February 1916. He carried messages with great bravery and success during the whole of the actions at Ypres, Festubert and Givenchy. In all his work he has consistently shown a disregard for danger and his faithfulness to duty is highly commendable.[29]

Pegahmagabow's service record reveals that he reverted back to the rank of private on September 14, 1916, ostensibly at his own request. Less than two weeks later, he was in the 2nd Southern General Hospital in Bristol, England, with a bullet wound to the left leg.[30]

On September 22, the 1st Battalion attacked the German lines east of Courcelette and, in heavy fighting, captured and held sections of the front-line trenches.[31] Pegahmagabow's service record is silent on why he opted for a reduction in rank a week before his battalion marched into the Courcelette sector, as well as the circumstances under which he was wounded. Clearly, the old Ojibwa medicine had failed him briefly.

Five months after being wounded, apparently badly enough that surgeons considered amputation, Pegahmagabow was itching to get back into the fighting and was complaining bitterly about being held back in England, where there was great temptation for wounded soldiers, with time on their hands, to indulge in whisky. "The reality of soldiering is nothing to me, although I had 20 months under shell fire in France, which I found not half as bad as it is back here in England," Pegahmagabow wrote to the secretary of Indian Affairs in March 1917. "Awarded a medal last June. I want another one while I have a chance."[32]

"Francis Pegahmagabow, after grabbing one medal, being wounded and recovered is back in France after a DCM," trumpeted

Isaac Rice (back row, centre) enlisted in the 162nd Battalion at Parry Sound in January 1916 and eventually reached the fighting in France as a reinforcement for the 1st Battalion, CEF, in May 1917. Severely wounded in the right arm in the assault on Passchendaele, he was invalided to England where he spent the remainder of the war. (*David L. Thomas Collection / Wasauksing First Nation, Tray 1-9*)

William Ireland in the *North Star* in December 1916.[33] In fact, it was May 1917 before Pegahmagabow returned to the 1st Battalion in France, having missed the massive Canadian assault on Vimy Ridge a month earlier. He was, however, greeted by a familiar face, that of fellow Parry Island band member Isaac (Menomenee) Rice, who had originally enlisted in the 162nd Battalion in Parry Sound in January 1916.[34]

About a year and a half into the war, Prime Minister Robert Borden announced Canada's armed forces were to be doubled in size to half a million men. Three divisions of volunteers were already wallowing in the mud of Europe by the end of 1915, but two more divisions were planned.

In order to increase enlistment, Sir Sam, as the minister of Militia and Defence, Sir Sam Hughes, was now known, devised a plan of making each county or district into a battalion recruiting area. The idea was that friends and neighbours would enlist together, knowing that they would be going overseas as a group. To heighten the feelings of camaraderie, prominent local citizens were appointed as officers. The Parry Sound-based 162nd Battalion under the command of MP James Arthurs, like nearly three-quarters of the 170 units authorized under the minister's local recruiting initiative, was broken up upon reaching England and its recruits dispersed to other units already in combat and badly in need of reinforcements.[35]

Recruiting officers did not bypass the native reserves, and the Parry Island council made numerous protests to Indian Affairs about their conduct. In April 1917, Councillor John Menomenee, Isaac Rice's father, made a motion that Indian Affairs be asked to use its influence to see that natives were no longer coerced into volunteering for military service.[36]

The 1st Battalion moved back into the Ypres salient early in November 1917 to take part in the assault on Passchendaele. From late October, the 3rd and 4th Canadian Divisions had crawled their way from one shell crater to the next, to within a quarter-mile of the top of the ridge. The second phase called for the 1st and 2nd Divisions to push forward with artillery support and overrun the German positions.

On November 1, Pegahmagabow was promoted corporal as his battalion prepared for the attack. Before moving to Passchendaele, all the soldiers of the 1st Division had undergone intensive practice in exercising initiative in unforeseen situations. Noncommissioned officers and senior privates were given opportunities to handle a platoon so that, in the event of casualties, no confusion would occur.[37]

In storming the ridge, Pegahmagabow unquestionably took charge and his diligence was recognized with the second award of the Military Medal. The citation reads:

> *At Passchendaele November 6/7, 1917, this NCO did excellent work. Before and after the attack he kept in touch with the flanks advising units he had seen, this information proving the success of the attack and saving time in consolidating. He also guided the relief to its proper place after it had become mixed up.*[38]

Years after the war, Pegahmagabow wrote about the attack on Passchendaele, which had been under cover of a creeping barrage advancing at a rate of fifty yards every four minutes. Unfortunately, Pegahmagabow claimed, shells were being lobbed into the German forward positions even after the positions had been overrun by the Canadians. As he informed the Department of National Defence in 1934,

> *At our objective we suffered very heavy from our own gunfire, I done all I could to stop it by reporting to our C.O. [commanding officer, Lieutenant-Colonel Albert Walter] Sparling and the artillery observers. My comrades going up in pieces, shell after shell. I had no relatives at home. I was only fighting for my comrades. At daylight cannonade was still going strong. Presence of mind came*

TOP The battlefield at Passchendaele, November 1917. *(Library and Archives Canada, PA-2084)*

BOTTOM Stretcher-bearers on the way to an aid post during the Battle of Passchendaele, November 1917. *(Library and Archives Canada, PA-2140)*

to me. I had a flare pistol with me. I shot a white flare. Millions of eyes saw it. It should have been fired when we reach our objective anyway ... The moment I shot the flare, field guns cease fire.[39]

Shortly before Christmas 1917, Pegahmagabow sought medical attention at 22 Casualty Clearing Station, and doctors diagnosed him as dangerously ill with pneumonia. Invalided back to England, he spent several months convalescing in military hospitals at Etaples, Colchester, and Epsom.

Posted to Bramshott camp, in the Aldershott area, for toughening up before returning to the trenches, Pegahmagabow bumped into 1st Battalion transport driver Corporal Roy Macfie, MM and bar, who had been wounded in the assault of Passchendaele and then hospitalized for laryngitis. In later years, Roy fondly recalled for his son John how Pegahmagabow had refused to take part in parade square drill, scornfully telling the sergeant that he had been fighting in the trenches before the disciplinarian had even joined up. In the place of exercise and drill, he was marched off to the stockade.[40]

A letter written to Pegahmagabow by an English civilian in April 1918 suggests that by this time he was also developing a resentment about the way natives were viewed and treated, a feeling he carried back to Canada with him and which grew over time. Cecilia Oldmeadow wrote:

I am quite sure no civilian in England or Canada (unless they are German agents) would say so wicked a thing as "them dogs let them suffer, take the money away from them, and kick them out." The civilians love and admire the splendid men who are fighting for them. You say a Red Indian is "a dummy and not to be trusted about the country ..."

From a child I was taught that the Red Indian was "the noble Red Man" and so believe most of the English. I loved above all things to be told by my father about Hiawatha. The white man has

*never despised the Red Indian. You are mistaken if you think so,
and you should be worthy of that title "the noble Red Man." When
we are truly noble we forgive injuries. So forgive and forget all
that has pained you ...*[41]

Pegahmagabow was back with his battalion in France in early
May 1918, well before the August 8 start of the massive Ami-
ens offensive, during which the 1st Battalion was held in brigade
reserve while the 2nd, 3rd, and 4th Battalions participated in the
4:20 a.m. attack. The 1st Battalion advanced one hour after the
attack began, but was not required to render assistance to the
assaulting troops. On the afternoon of the following day, however,
the 1st Battalion's "C" Company cleared the enemy from the
southern portion of the village of Beaufort while "A" Company
captured the village of Folies and took about sixty prisoners. During the operation, the battalion captured sixteen enemy machine
guns, two anti-tank guns, and two mortars.[42] Overall, the Canadian Corps advanced eight miles and took over 5,000 prisoners.

The Battle of the Scarpe, part of Second Arras, began on August
26. Four days later, the 1st, 2nd, and 3rd battalions attacked at 4:20
a.m. through heavy machine-gun fire. Although prisoners were
taken early in the assault and the 1st Brigade was able to report at
9:20 a.m. that all objectives had been attained, the enemy counter-
attacked in force just over two hours later. "Artillery and machine-
gun fire from the enemy's position made it virtually impossible to
evacuate the wounded during the day and much delay was experienced in getting messages through by runner," wrote Captain
Walter Bennett Durward. The 1st Battalion suffered 167 casualties,
including seven officers, in the engagement.[43]

It was during the fighting on August 30 that Pegahmagabow
earned the second bar to his Military Medal. Lieutenant-Colonel
Sparling, the 1st Battalion's commanding officer, detailed the circumstances in his recommendation, written on September 8:

During the operations on August 30th, 1918, at Orix Trench, near Upton Wood, when his company were almost out of ammunition and in danger of being surrounded, this NCO went over the top under heavy MG [machine gun] and rifle fire and brought back sufficient ammunition to enable the post to carry on and assist in repulsing heavy enemy counter-attacks.[44]

Although Pegahmagabow had won the Military Medal a third time, he was clearly not the same soldier who had first set foot on French soil in 1915. Three years of shelling and butchery in the trenches had seemingly begun to take its toll. Discipline became a problem, Pegahmagabow believing that his company sergeant-major was persecuting him by continually assigning him work when their battalion was not in combat. He insisted the sergeant-major did not know his own duties, and complained to his company commander about the way he was being treated.[45]

After several peculiar incidents, concerned superiors ordered Pegahmagabow to report to No. 1 Canadian Field Ambulance on September 12, 1918, for observation. On one occasion, he apparently held a Canadian medical officer at gunpoint and accused him of being a German spy because he was near a well and yet had no instrument for testing the water. Another time, he flatly refused an order from his sergeant-major to change his post because it was not put into writing.[46]

Although written in 1932 and not in 1918, a letter Pegahmagabow sent to his first commanding officer, Brigadier-General Frederic Hill, clearly reflects a shift in attitude towards his officers by the final year of the war.[47] Apparently, Pegahmagabow had little regard for Lieutenant-Colonel Sparling, a 26-year-old farmer from Saskatchewan. As a company commander in the 10th Battalion, Sparling won the DSO at Vimy Ridge for tackling and disarming an enemy sniper.[48] Given a promotion and command of the 1st Battalion just four months after his heroics at Vimy,

Canadian Corps commander Sir Arthur Currie and the Duke of Connaught (former Canadian governor general) inspect the 1st Canadian Infantry Battalion, June 1918. *(Library and Archives Canada, PA-2760)*

Sparling earned two bars to his DSO for outstanding leadership of his new battalion. In his letter to Hill, Pegahmagabow said:

Col. Sparling, he had it in for me and used me like a dozen men. Half my reports he would not believe them. I did not think much of him. Most of my time I engage myself in sniping so he could not find me when he wanted me. He nearly got captured one night and lost all the scout section after he deny my report of our front... I done all I could for Col. Sparling, but I could never please him.[49]

Pegahmagabow was invalided to England in early November and bounced from one military hospital to the next while doctors tried to determine what, if anything, was wrong with him. By November 11, the day the armistice took effect, doctors at Lord Derby War Hospital in Warrington had officially given their diagnosis as "exhaustion psychosis."[50]

In April 1919, Pegahmagabow was back in Canada, this time a patient at St. Andrew's Military Hospital in Toronto. Doctors finally recommended that he be discharged to civilian life a month later.

CHAPTER 3

The Returned Hero

DURING THE SPRING of 1919, dozens of local boys were stepping off the trains in Parry Sound, returning from the fighting overseas. Despite the numbers of khaki figures filling the town's streets, Pegahmagabow didn't escape the scrutiny of the *North Star*'s new editor, John Schofield Dick, who made note of his arrival. The ever-smiling Peggy, always desirous of attention, told the engrossed newsman how he had sniped an astounding 378 Germans at the front. While he stated that he had won the MM and two bars, he also fibbed a little and claimed to have been recommended for the Victoria Cross.[1]

There can be little doubt that members of the Parry Island band initially greeted Pegahmagabow as a great warrior and hero in the

FACING PAGE In 1906, John Wanamaker, owner of the Wanamaker department stores of Philadelphia and New York, hired Joseph Kossuth Dixon to give daily lectures in a 3,000-seat auditorium illustrated with slides and motion pictures. Beginning in 1908, Rodman Wanamaker, son of the owner, sponsored a series of photographic expeditions to numerous Indian reservations of the western United States. Following the First World War, Dixon began documenting American Indian participation in the U.S. military. It remains somewhat of a mystery how this portrait of Cpl. Francis Pegahmagabow, taken by Parry Sound studio photographer William John Boyd, came to be part of the Wanamaker collection. (*Wanamaker Collection W7679 / Mathers Museum, Indiana University*)

tradition of their forefathers. Just over a month after his discharge from the military, Pegahmagabow exchanged vows with 17-year-old Eva Tronche in a marriage arranged by her father, Elijah, a French trapper married to Mary Nanibush. Tronche had practised and performed as a musician with Francis before the war.[2]

While Chief Peter Megis and the Parry Island band council had reacted favourably to Pegahmagabow's enlistment, even offering a donation from band funds to his unit in September 1914, the activities of recruiters to compel young men to volunteer in the years afterward had created open hostility.[3]

According to letters of protest from the chief and council, Simpson John Manitowaba and Henry Medwayosh were coerced into enlisting in the 162nd Battalion at Parry Sound in January 1916, although both were underage. They subsequently deserted in October 1916, while the battalion was undergoing basic training at Niagara-on-the-Lake, Ontario, and made their way home to the sanctuary of their reserve.[4] Medwayosh was sheltered by his parents until the spring of 1918 when military authorities arrested him on Parry Island.[5]

Still, eager to recognize a hero, the Parry Island band paid the travelling expenses, in August 1919, for Pegahmagabow and his bride to go to Toronto, where the young veteran received his Military Medal and two bars directly from the Prince of Wales, the future King Edward VIII.[6] At a ceremony at the Canadian National Exhibition, he was one of almost 200 veterans decorated before a crowd estimated at 50,000 by the Toronto newspapers. Boasting, or perhaps being truthful, Pegahmagabow told reporters that he had done in 378 of the enemy with his rifle.[7]

Both the Toronto media and the *North Star* made much of the meeting between the warrior Pegahmagabow and the prince:

It was one of the stirring moments of the great fair and the crowd cheered lustily the brave redman, whose doughty deeds thrilled an army... Sturdy, well set up and with soldierly brevity, he thanked his future sovereign, as his decoration was pinned to his breast. His people watched the scene with interested eyes. It must have been one of the proudest moments of their lives and it is a tribute to British justice that those who dwell under the flag, be they redman or black, come to love it and are willing to die for it as their own.[8]

Eager to show how much Canada's aboriginal communities had contributed to the war effort, Indian Affairs lapped up the newspaper accounts of Pegahmagabow's overseas service and reprinted

Henry Medwayosh joined the 162nd Battalion in Parry Sound in January 1916, although his parents told authorities repeatedly that he was under-age and did not have their permission to enlist. *(David L. Thomas Collection / Wasauksing First Nation, Tray 2-2)*

the published details in the department's official *Annual Report For The Year Ended March 31, 1919*.[9] This was to prove an embarrassment to the government years later when Pegahmagabow turned up on Parliament Hill demonstrating for the exemption of natives from income tax and conscription. Reporters seeking information about the Indian with all the medals were elated when clerks at Indian Affairs brought forth the annual report showing him to be a genuine hero.

While Pegahmagabow may have been loose-lipped about his wartime exploits during the summer of 1919, numerous band elders and acquaintances, as well as his son Duncan, concur that he rarely spoke about his experiences in the trenches. "He was a quiet man, he was a real gentleman," recalled 84-year-old Lyle Jones, who worked with Pegahmagabow during the 1940s, in a 1991 interview. "He could have been a boastful man for what he did. But to my knowledge he never said a word about it."[10]

Once the publicity over his war record died down, Pegahmagabow settled into life on the reserve. It was a rude awakening. As a soldier, he had found that the horrors of life in the trenches quickly submerged distinctions based on class, religion, politics, or race, and, like other returning soldiers, Pegahmagabow had brought with him the fervent hope that postwar Canada would be a better place because of their sacrifices. Instead, many who had enlisted from well-paying jobs found themselves working for little more than their $1.10-a-day army pay, while their replacements had prospered on rising wartime wages. The special programs instituted for former soldiers scarcely helped the dismal employment picture.

As a returned soldier, Francis Pegahmagabow faced the added disadvantage of being an Indian. Deprived of much of the game and fish on which their traditional economy depended, Parry Sound-area aboriginals had also found that the poor quality of their reserve lands denied them a living based on cultivation of the soil. At the same time, they had been only partially integrated into the economy of the dominant society as seasonal labourers for the lumber companies and as guides. Others, such as Richard King, danced on the government wharf in Parry Sound dressed in his traditional attire in return for handouts from tourists.

On top of everything else, Pegahmagabow started to suffer a decline in health almost from the time of his discharge. Shortly after his discharge in May 1919, he was admitted to the hospital in Parry Sound complaining of chest pains. He was finally released after a month of bed rest and the problem was diagnosed as an enlarged heart, likely caused by his bout with pneumonia. While a doctor advised the Board of Pension Commissioners that he suffered from a thirty-per-cent disability, Pegahmagabow was denied a pension because there didn't appear to have been anything wrong with him at the time of discharge. The board argued "there has been nothing brought forward to show this enlargement was due to service."[11]

Initially, the local Indian agent, Alexander Logan, secured employment for Pegahmagabow, first as a fire ranger during the hot summer months and later cutting railway ties for the Canadian National Railway during the winter.[12] However, as a result of his apparent physical limitations, Pegahmagabow's primary employment came from guiding vacationing anglers during the summer months and hunters in the autumn, although he did sail on the Department of Marine and Fisheries ship *Grenville* for a time.

It's clear that after giving up more than four years of his life in service to his country, Pegahmagabow felt it owed him something more. This brought him into conflict with Logan, who felt the Indian should be happy with what he had and stop bothering him.

A hardware merchant, undertaker, fire chief, and one of the first builders in Parry Sound, the Scottish-born Logan treated his employment as Indian agent as superfluous. Indian Affairs fre-

Francis Pegahmagabow frequently worked as a fishing guide for guests at the nearby Rose Point Hotel. This photo was taken prior to renovations following a January 1918 fire. *(David L. Thomas Collection / Archives of Ontario, C 253 Tray 7-28)*

quently complained that he did not answer his correspondence in time, neglected to forward Indian band council resolutions, ignored instructions from the Department, and often could not account properly for money advanced to him for expenses. During the war, his work became so bad that the Department sometimes did not pay his salary and threatened to replace him, if he did not "pay strict attention to [his] duties."[13]

During the summer of 1919, Pegahmagabow had several discussions with Logan about his future. While Pegahmagabow wanted to take out a rather large loan for a farm under the Soldier Settlement Act of 1919, Logan tried repeatedly to dissuade him. In

Hardware merchant, undertaker, and fire chief Alexander Logan was also one of the first builders in Parry Sound. Appointed Indian agent of the Parry Sound superintendency in March 1912, Logan was dismissed in September 1922. *(Dora Taylor Logan)*

October, Pegahmagabow wrote directly to the Soldiers Aid Commission complaining that Logan was not helping him.[14]

Chastised by Indian Affairs, Logan replied that he could not and would not encourage Pegahmagabow to go into farming. Instead, Logan claimed that he had advised Pegahmagabow to get a few acres near the village and start a small market garden. The Department could possibly help with a small loan to help him to get a horse and a cow.[15] Logan wrote to his superiors in January 1920:

This man is very hard to handle as he suffers from dementia and takes very strange notions. When he came home last May I looked after him and had him appointed fire ranger on Parry Island. About the time he was to start he took sick and went to the hospital in Parry Sound, was there three weeks and when he got out of bed he slipped away of his own accord and got married a week later to an Indian girl... I will not encourage him to go farming for the only reason I can see to his going farming is that he thinks he can get a loan of $1,500 or $2,000 and have plenty of money to spend...[16]

When Logan finally submitted Pegahmagabow's application, he did all he could to undermine its acceptance, insisting Pegahmagabow was disabled with dementia and that the site was in a "most out of the way place for a successful farmer." Enclosed with the application was a letter from band councillor Elijah Tabobondung stating that Pegahmagabow had received a great deal of money following his discharge, but had squandered it all.[17] Clearly jealous, Tabobondung wrote that Pegahmagabow didn't deserve anything under the Soldier Settlement Act. With the local agent, its man in the field, so to speak, advising strongly against a loan for Pegahmagabow, Indian Affairs naturally refused his application.

In October 1920, the Parry Island band council passed a resolution that Pegahmagabow be granted a loan to purchase a team of horses, a wagon, and harnesses, and this time Logan initially offered his support, recommending a loan of $450 to his superiors. Three weeks later, Logan seemed to have had a change of heart, advising approval be deferred until the spring to avoid the cost of maintaining the horses through the winter. He noted that hay cost $38 a ton and Pegahmagabow was already $300 in debt. Finally, Indian Affairs withheld approval after Logan wrote:

He is a returned soldier and thinks we should help him and while I would like to do all I can for him, he is not very well balanced and does not make good at anything and I am afraid he will be the same in his farming venture.[18]

By 1921, Chief Peter Megis had been the political leader of the Parry Island band for almost twenty-five years. In February of that year, Pegahmagabow defeated the old chief and one other candidate, Joseph Partridge, to take up the reins of power on the island.[19] Chief Megis passed away just two months later, after a brief illness.

While Indian Affairs generally praised the work of Chief Megis, the chief and his council had been under fire from a progressive wing within the band since 1918 for impeding development. This

Parry Sound Indian agent Alexander Logan (centre) with Parry Island band members (from left) David Hawk, Thomas Medwayosh, Chief Peter Megis, and David Menomenee. *(David L. Thomas Collection / Wasauksing First Nation, Tray 1-43)*

faction described Megis as the head of a family compact intent on preserving absolute power on the reserve. Eventually, Pegahmagabow found himself facing the same sort of opposition.

Parry Island had changed greatly during the time that Megis had been chief. In 1895 the band had reluctantly surrendered a 325-acre right-of-way across the reserve to Ottawa lumberman John Rudolphus Booth, providing his ambitious Canada Atlantic Railway with a western terminus on Georgian Bay.[20] Within a couple of years, the facilities at Depot Harbour included a massive million-bushel grain elevator, over 2,000 feet of dock space, and extensive freight sheds and warehouses. In 1899, Booth was able to expropriate a further 110 acres of reserve land to build residences

With single and duplex homes, boarding houses, stores, school, hotel, and three churches, the railway community of Depot Harbour on Parry Island boasted a population of over 600 by the 1911 census. (*David L. Thomas Collection / Archives of Ontario, C 253, Tray 5-16*)

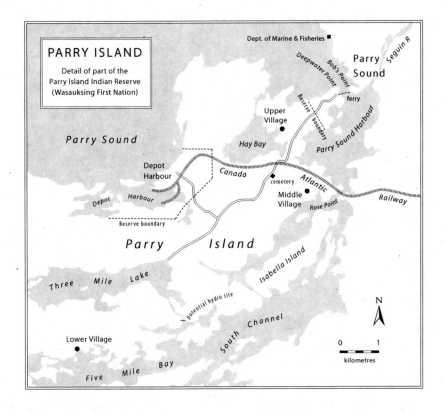

PARRY ISLAND
Detail of part of the
Parry Island Indian Reserve
(Wasauksing First Nation)

for the railway employees, after the band steadfastly refused to a voluntary sale. Soon this townsite boasted numerous single and duplex homes, boarding houses, stores, a school, three churches, and a hotel.

Inevitably, the railway and its employees had a major impact on the Parry Island Indian community. By the 1920s, members of other bands who flocked to Parry Island for seasonal work at Depot Harbour made up nearly two-thirds of the island's aboriginal population. A few settled permanently on Parry Island, marrying into the band or joining other family members already settled.

The resolutions passed by Pegahmagabow's council frequently had no effect. Sometimes they were simply not passed on by the local Indian agent to his superiors in Ottawa, or the bureaucrats in Ottawa advised against what the democratically elected band council had decided. Sometimes Pegahmagabow was affected personally. In April 1921, the band council, now under Pegahmagabow's leadership, passed another resolution that he be granted a loan for a team of horses. Pegahmagabow didn't get his loan after Logan advised his superiors, "I have been trying to show him the utter foolishness of going into more debt and advised him to clean up a few acres and put it in good shape…"[21]

The refusal by Indian Affairs to approve the loans granted to Pegahmagabow by the Parry Island band council is probably what triggered the running feud between the veteran and the paternalistic Department of Indian Affairs that carried on for the next three decades. While Pegahmagabow wanted Indian Affairs to respect the will of the band council, the local Indian agent and his superiors expected him to take on a subordinate position. Pegahmagabow's personal papers reflect a conviction that he had a "God-given duty" to "save my tribes from slavery."[22]

One of the first things Pegahmagabow did as chief was try to regain ownership of a 2.75-acre parcel of reserve land that had been purchased under unusual circumstances by former Parry Sound MP John Galna and his brother-in-law and business partner, Robert Danter.[23] At a special meeting of the Parry Island council in June 1921, Pegahmagabow got the ball rolling with a resolution to buy the land back using money from the band's capital funds.

In 1900, longtime Methodist missionary Allen Salt had obtained a 93.5-acre parcel from the band on which to retire. Galna and Danter apparently visited the elderly minister in 1902 while his sons were away and convinced him to sell the land, on which the shipping partners had illegally constructed boathouses, docks, an ice house, a work shop, a blacksmith shop, storehouses, and even a residence, perhaps as early as 1895. The sale of the land by Salt was viewed as a betrayal by members of the Parry Island band and created a bitterness between them and the missionary's descendants that lasted for decades.

After Galna's death in 1918, his heirs wanted to dispose of the property and Pegahmagabow clearly wanted the band to get it back. To Pegahmagabow, the land represented the loss of another portion of their island to white business interests, from which they gained nothing. The property became the subject of numerous letters, meetings, and band council resolutions during the next four years, but Indian Affairs steadfastly refused to authorize the purchase.

The soundness of Pegahmagabow's initiative became evident in August 1934 when Charles and Roy Salt purchased the property, along with a 2.76-acre water lot, from Galna's daughter for $1,200.[24] By then there were numerous vehicles on Parry Island, primarily owned by residents of Depot Harbour, but without access to the mainland. The Galna property at Deepwater Point, the closest part of the reserve to Parry Sound, became the obvious site for a profitable ferry business, which operated into the 1950s.

Protecting the rights and property of the community was of the utmost importance to Pegahmagabow. Although the Canada Atlantic Railway had been required to erect solid fences along the right-of-way and install cattle guards on its locomotives to prevent livestock from being hurt, the company failed to keep up repair of the fences, leading to numerous claims from Parry Island residents for loss of livestock, which were paid. The disrepair of the fences led to Parry Island cattle wandering into Depot Harbour, where they were impounded, and Depot Harbour cattle getting on to the reserve, where they destroyed Indian gardens. The matter became complicated in 1905 when Depot Harbour and the right-of-way became the property of the Grand Trunk Railway (which in turn was taken over by the federal government in 1918 and later became part of the Canadian National Railway).

The lack of fencing was discussed at a special council meeting in May 1923, and a month later council passed a resolution requesting that Indian Affairs see to it that the terms of the original 1896 surrender to the Canada Atlantic Railway were honoured. The resolution noted that Parry Island residents at that point did not receive compensation for dead livestock. A letter to Indian Affairs followed in June 1925, indicating that nothing had become of the resolution.[25]

Given the band's previous experience with expropriation, Pegahmagabow was hesitant to explore business opportunities that involved any sort of intrusion onto the reserve by outside parties, especially for the development of natural resources. During the early twentieth century, the Department of Indian Affairs granted permission to dozens of individuals and companies to prospect for minerals on Parry Island, but none discovered more than trace amounts of gold and copper. This changed in February 1921 when the *North Star* reported on the front page that a garnet and mica deposit had been discovered close to Depot Harbour and a large-scale mine would soon open.[26] Extensive testing by the Department of Mines confirmed that minerals lay under the railway property at Depot Harbour, but the larger deposits were to be found on the Indian reserve.

Determined that the band would benefit fully from any mining operation, Pegahmagabow consulted a lawyer. There are indications that Robert A. Bryce of the Garnet Abrasives Corporation Ltd. intended to build a concentrator on the railway property, providing that access mining would also extend onto the reserve, "but apparently the Indians were inimical to the project."[27]

Pegahmagabow and the council also sought the cancellation of a licence granted in 1921 to the Canadian National Lumber and Tie Company to cut timber on the reserve, claiming the company exceeded the area assigned to it and refused work to aboriginal men while whites were given preference. Although council passed a resolution in June 1923 requesting that the licence be cancelled, Indian Affairs took no action.[28] Apparently, the cutting continued for years to come, until the company itself halted operations because all the valuable timber had been removed.

Although appearing to always be revisting old grievances, Pegahmagabow could also be progressive. In the spring of 1925, he corresponded with the Boving Hydraulic and Engineering Co. about building a small hydroelectric plant on a creek on Parry Island, capable of delivering upwards of fourteen horsepower (10.4 kilowatts)—perhaps enough to power the homes of reserve residents.[29] Council took a first step towards implementing the idea by passing a resolution to install electric lighting in the public buildings using band funds, but Indian Affairs would not approve. "In view of the fact that the buildings are not used to any extent at night, it is considered that the department would not be justified in incurring the large expense which would result from having a lighting plant installed," wrote the acting assistant deputy minister, A.F. Mackenzie.[30]

Other than through band council resolutions, there were few avenues for aboriginals to try to effect change. One was the Grand General Indian Council of Ontario—the Grand Council—where delegates primarily reviewed federal Indian legislation and made recommendations for changes, although few had any impact. "At council, delegates honed their leadership skills, obtained a wider knowledge of Anishinabek history, became mindful of the broader implications of federal legislation and exchanged practical solutions to common problems," one scholar recently wrote.[31] In forwarding a Parry Island resolution for band funds to cover host expenses, Indian agent Logan declared the delegates "had a big time. I do not know whether their meetings are good but it seems to please some of them."[32]

While the Department of Indian Affairs did provide Grand Council presidents or secretaries with responses to Grand Council resolutions and usually approved the travelling expenses of delegates from band funds, there was a feeling that not much was being accomplished. At a Grand Council Meeting of Mohawks in Oshweken in December 1918, the Oliver Act (on the sale of Indian lands) came under strong criticism, and it was decided that a province-wide and, preferably, nationwide political organization was needed to represent Indians. Frederick Ogilvie Loft was elected president and given the task of building the organization, named the League of Indians of Ontario.[33]

Loft was a Six Nations Mohawk who had both served overseas as a lieutenant and worked to recruit natives for the military. An educated man, employed as an accountant-clerk at the Asylum for the Insane in Toronto, he had met privately with King George V while in England. Still, he was not held in high regard by the head of Indian Affairs, Duncan Campbell Scott, who wrote:

> *He has some education, has a rather attractive personal appearance, but he is a shallow, talkative individual. He is one of the few Indians who are endeavouring to live off their brethren by organizing an Indian society, and collecting fees from them ... He volunteered for the war and looked very well in uniform, but he was cunning enough to evade any active service, and I do not think his record in that regard is a very good one.*[34]

Logan used an apparent smallpox outbreak as a guise to stop the delegates from Parry Island and Magnetewan from attending the founding convention of the League of Indians of Ontario in Sault Ste. Marie, Ontario, in September 1919. When Logan later forwarded resolutions passed by the Henvey Inlet and Shawanaga band councils to pay the expenses of their delegates from band funds, Indian Affairs refused, pointing out that approval had not been obtained prior to the convention.[35]

The Department of Indian Affairs clearly viewed the League of Indians of Ontario as a threat and did whatever possible to undermine Loft and his organization. Scott at one point considered silencing Loft by enfranchising him—in effect taking away his Indian status. Loft's routine appeals for donations for paper,

Frederick Ogilvie Loft, from a painting by Andrew R. Hughes.
(*Dr. Donald B. Smith*)

stamps, and other expenses from various Indian bands eventually presented Indian Affairs with a way to keep him quiet. A 1927 amendment to the Indian Act made it illegal to solicit funds from Indians or bands without permission from Indian Affairs. Loft was threatened by Indian Affairs with imprisonment after he wrote bands in 1931 soliciting contributions for himself and a law-yer to go to England and test, before the Privy Council, the legal-ity of provincial hunting laws that were restricting Indian hunting rights.

Pegahmagabow met Loft on June 9, 1921, when Loft came to a

gathering in the Parry Sound council chambers, which included representatives from Parry Island, Shawanaga, Cape Croker and Longlac.[36] Although it wasn't until February 1922 that the Parry Island council passed a resolution to join the League of Indians, Pegahmagabow was clearly taken with Loft's ideas.[37] Early in 1922 he wrote to Loft:

> *I may say we have the influence of the people although I have not been able to obtain money to cover the small fee. I could have paid it long before, but I was prohibited to pay it out of my own pocket till the League itself well understood by the band. I have full confidence in the League as it is our only hope to consolidate our land title...*[38]

It wasn't very long after meeting Loft that Pegahmagabow began his own crusade to unite the Parry Island, Shawanaga, Magnetewan and French River bands in voicing their common grievances against Indian Affairs. Clearly, not always sure of his facts, Pegahmagabow began "rocking the boat" on a series of issues that caused no end of anxiety for John McLean Daly, who had been appointed the new Indian agent at Parry Sound after Indian Affairs finally dismissed Alexander Logan in September 1922.[39]

In a 1991 interview, band elder James Edward Wheatley, 89, illustrated the relationship between Pegahmagabow and Daly by banging his two clenched fists together. "Oh they were always at each other's throats," Wheatley explained. "Mr. Daly rubbed him wrong and Francis reciprocated."[40]

Born in Scotland in 1873, Daly had worked as a police constable for the Temiskaming and Northern Ontario Railway in North Bay for seven years. He had enlisted in 1915 and served in France with the Canadian Overseas Railway Construction Corps, rising quickly to the rank of sergeant.[41] In March 1918, he was granted a furlough to Canada after his wife, Margaret, died suddenly at age 45 from cancer, leaving six young children without anyone to care

John McLean Daly served overseas with the Canadian Expeditionary Force, and later as Indian agent at Parry Sound, Sept. 1922 to Sept. 1938. *(Royal Canadian Legion, Pioneer Branch 117)*

for them.[42] Appointed Indian agent in Parry Sound after briefly working for the Customs Department, Daly married Parry Island school teacher Edith Helena Smiley in 1927, with whom he had another two children.[43]

An article in the *Journal of the Canadian Historical Association* gives detailed insight into Daly's character:

[He was] a peremptory, rather self-important man concerned to maintain his position in the hierarchy, genuinely interested in "helping" aboriginal people along the lines laid down by the Department of Indian Affairs, but an active opponent of any initiative

John McLean Daly (with cane) and his wife, Edith, with members of the
Parry Island band at the 1927 Canadian National Exhibition in Toronto.
(David L. Thomas Collection / Archives of Ontario, C 253 Tray 18-8)

*among native people to assert control over their own affairs. Daly's
attitude towards First Nations was one of superiority, which took a
patronizing but benign form toward those who appeared to accept
his authority, and led to sincere outrage when his right to rule was
questioned.*[44]

In her study of the relationships between the First Nations communities of Parry Island and Wikwemikong with their respective

Indian agents between the two world wars, Robin Jarvis Brownlie wrote that Daly's writings "depict the leaders as irrational, petty, foolish, and self-serving—a prime technique of DIA officials to dismiss aboriginal spokespersons. Daly portrayed the grievances they raised as mere pretexts for posturing and self-aggrandizement."[45] In the case of Pegahmagabow, Daly was also able to exploit the veteran's alleged dementia to undermine legitimate complaints. In one letter, Daly advised his superiors: "I should state that the general belief of whites as well as Indians in this district is that Pegahmagabow is not quite right in the head."[46]

It's important to note that Pegahmagabow was not the only Ojibwa in the southeastern corner of Georgian Bay who Daly found to be troublesome. There was also Henry Jackson of Christian Island, characterized by Daly as "the laziest Indian between Georgian Bay and Hudson's Bay," and Henry Abetung of Shawanaga, who Daly threatened with jail or "a sock in the eye" on several occasions. Although aboriginal lawyer and legal historian Paul Williams referred to all three men as "returned soldier chiefs," there are no CEF personnel files for Abetung and Jackson. The latter in fact served as assistant secretary of the Grand General Indian Council of Ontario from 1916 until he was elected president in 1918.[47]

During the summer of 1923, Pegahmagabow visited the various bands along Georgian Bay as far as the lower French River trying to get them to co-operate on a petition of grievances that would bypass Indian Affairs and go directly to King George V. Daly passed on word of Pegahmagabow's "seditious campaigning" to Indian Affairs, who advised the agent to "intimate" that his conduct could result in him being deposed as chief for incompetence. "This course is thought more advisable than a direct letter from the Department to the chief which might convey to him an exaggerated conception of the importance of his activities," Indian Affairs counselled Daly in 1924.[48]

Pegahmagabow seems to have ignored Daly's warnings or more

likely they increased his determination. "I try to explain to him that he must get in line…," Daly wrote. "To mention the Department to him is like tossing a red flag to a bull. Had I not a little experience with the disgruntled returned man, I would be justified in being nervous."[49]

By the summer of 1925, Pegahmagabow realized that he wasn't getting anywhere and a white lawyer might help him get recognition. This was a tactic endorsed by Chief Peter Megis as early as 1918 when Parry Island, Shawanaga, and Magnetewan gave band funds to Orillia solicitor J. Hugh Hammond so he could go to Ottawa on their behalf to press a claim that they had not ceded their rights to the Georgian Bay islands in the Robinson Huron Treaty of 1850.

Pegahmagabow's grievances against Indian Affairs captured the interest of Parry Sound lawyer John Roland Hett, himself a returned soldier who had been so seriously wounded in the back of his head by shellfire in 1917 that he'd been unable to walk or talk for a year.[50] Hett had resumed his studies at Osgoode Hall Law School and was called to the Ontario bar in June 1919 at age 27, thanks in large part to the waiving of school and articling requirements for veterans. A lawyer clearly drawn to causes, the flamboyant Hett made newspaper headlines across the province in 1928 for defending an American fugitive accused of killing an area farmer in a shootout.[51] Although a Parry Sound jury found his client guilty and he was sentenced to hang, Hett argued the case all the way to the Supreme Court of Canada, ostensibly without any remuneration.

Probably most horrifying to Indian Affairs was Pegahmagabow's contention that the Parry Island band had been swindled out of the sixteen-square-mile tract allocated to them by the Robinson Huron Treaty of 1850, and which had become the site of the town of Parry Sound.[52] An 1853 order-in-council had substituted Parry Island, measuring some 18,500 acres (about twenty-nine square miles), for the original reserve site at the mouth of the

During the early 1920s, Chief Francis Pegahmagabow's grievances against Indian Affairs captured the interest of flamboyant Parry Sound lawyer John Roland Hett, who had served in France as a lieutenant in the 1st North Midland Brigade, Royal Field Artillery. A 1927 amendment to the Indian Act barred Indians from soliciting funds to hire lawyers to fight claims cases unless the government approved. *(Kathleen Dooly)*

Seguin River. Pegahmagabow also told Hett that the native chiefs had not surrendered, and therefore still owned, all the islands in Georgian Bay. The islands were being used for cottage sites, and Pegahmagabow, John Manitowaba, and others felt that the Parry Island band should at least receive rent for these properties.

Although democratically elected chief, Pegahmagabow alienated a large number of the reserve's residents by suggesting to Indian Affairs that non-members of the band be removed, including the numerous children of Edward Wheatley, a white man married to an Indian woman ("Too many non-members, half-breeds, and white people on this reserve to contend with," he would later write).[53] Another cause for dissatisfaction was that Pegahmagabow was "inclined to be somewhat dictatorial." A memorandum suggested Pegahmagabow be advised to be "less arbitrary in his dealings with the Indians and refrain as much as possible from arousing hostility by any hasty or ill-considered action on his part."[54]

Stewart King, a 60-year-old band elder, suggested in a 2005 interview that Pegahmagabow's devout Roman Catholicism may also have been a strong factor in his conflicts with other band members, as the two religious factions lived in separate villages, the Upper Village at the northeastern corner of the island being Methodist, the Lower Village at the south end Catholic. "It wasn't that long ago that the United Church (Methodists) and the Catholics didn't get along and they always tried to keep them separate," he said.[55]

Almost from the time of the 1921 election, Councillor Johnson Tabobondung had been at odds with Pegahmagabow on numerous issues in the Parry Island council chamber. As early as December of that year, Alfred Tabobondung put together a petition to Indian Affairs to have Pegahmagabow removed as chief because he frequently gave permission for things without bringing them to council for a vote.[56]

Just as there had been accusations against Chief Megis that he was too autocratic and dictatorial, so too were the complaints about Pegahmagabow. Looking a little deeper, however, one sees that Councillor John Miller usually sided with Pegahmagabow in votes, frustrating Tabobondung and his supporters. Pegahmagabow's periodic outbursts of temper didn't help and, in fact, gave ammunition to those claiming he was incompetent, such as that displayed at a March 1922 council meeting in which he allegedly brandished a pearl-handled revolver.[57]

Pegahmagabow survived another petition to have him ousted

in December 1923 and was, in fact, re-elected chief two months later, soundly defeating Joseph Partridge, one of the men behind the petition. About the time Pegahmagabow began his association with Hett in the spring of 1925, yet another petition surfaced alleging he took bribes from trespassers to allow them to fish and pick berries on Indian land. The petitioners also claimed great dissatisfaction that he was spending time visiting lawyers instead of tending to his duties as chief.[58]

Clearly unhappy that Pegahmagabow had been re-elected chief and not looking forward to dealing with him for the next three years, Daly recommended to Indian Affairs that Pegahmagabow be removed as chief and Partridge be appointed in his place. Writing about an April 2 council meeting, at which the latest petition was discussed at length, he said:

> *The general conversation was that Francis Pegahmagabow, the whole time that he was chief was causing trouble and going to lawyers and defying the Department and causing the band to be dissatisfied with their lot and the Indian Department's method of running the reserves. The band doesn't want their chief to be going to other bands trying to cause trouble about treaties, which they think the Department is capable of looking after.[59]*

An appeal by Councillor John Miller that several of the signatures on the latest petition had been obtained by questionable means seems to have been ignored by Daly, who had made up his mind that Pegahmagabow was "of no value to me or to the band." Miller argued unsuccessfully that many band members had signed a blank paper to which the particulars were added later. These same people signed another petition that they were quite satisfied with how Pegahmagabow performed as chief.[60]

On advice from Indian Affairs, Daly set out to convince Pegahmagabow that he had become "unpopular" and secure his resignation. Pegahmagabow finally quit in August 1925, and although he ran for chief in the January 1926 election, he only received one vote—his own.[61]

It must have been a powerful blow to Pegahmagabow that his own band, the very people he was trying to help, had turned on him. With his overwhelming defeat, Pegahmagabow seemed to lose all interest in politics, even in native rights.

CHAPTER 4

The Disillusioned Veteran

NEARLY TWO DECADES after Edward, the Prince of Wales, had pinned the Military Medal and two bars to his chest, Pegahmagabow headed to Toronto to serve as a member of the veterans guard of honour during the 1939 royal visit of King George VI and Queen Elizabeth.[1] It's notable that while thousands of veterans saw the couple in communities across Canada during the first visit to the country by a reigning sovereign, most wore civilian dress clothes, their medals, and a red beret with a crown. Twenty years after the armistice, most veterans were happy to forget the war and get on with their civilian lives. Pegahmagabow, on the other hand, seems to have gone wearing his uniform. During the war, in an army of khaki-clad soldiers, differences in race and skin colour had been disregarded. The military was the one place where he had experienced equality and respect. In a third-person narrative he wrote later, Pegahmagabow captures how significant the uniform made him feel:

As a real soldier he really look smart and very important in uniform of sergeant-major, string of medals on his breast. He tried to cheer up a lady in grief who lost two sons in war. How people cheer when he come by the march past but he give his soldiers credit for that.[2]

During the fall of 1925, just after he resigned as chief of the Parry Island band, Pegahmagabow wrote to Brigadier-General Hill, who was now an instructor at the Royal Military College in Kingston, inquiring whether he could get back into the army. In his October 1925 reply, Hill was not optimistic, but claimed he would do what he could. In part, he wrote:

> *We who were privileged to serve in the old 1st Battalion remember your very good and faithful work and are very interested in your welfare. As to joining the army, I don't think you would better your position even if a suitable place could be found for you. Peacetime soldiering is not much like soldiering in war. Then there is the question of your age...*[3]

During the mid-1920s, Pegahmagabow joined "A" Company of the 23rd Northern Pioneers militia regiment stationed at Parry Sound. With companies of twenty-five noncommissioned officers and men at each of Parry Sound, North Bay, Huntsville, and Bracebridge, the regiment was a mere shadow of what it had been during the war years.[4] Unfortunately, there are no surviving pay lists or service files for Non-Permanent Active Militia after 1914, so Pegahmagabow's involvement remains hazy. It is known that he qualified for the rank of sergeant by the close of 1928 and company sergeant-major by the spring of 1930.

It's probable that Lieutenant-Colonel William James Lalor had a hand in getting Pegahmagabow involved in the militia in Parry Sound. In August 1914, Lalor, then a captain in the 23rd Northern Pioneers, brought eight volunteers from "E" Company in Utterson to the fairgrounds in Parry Sound. Out of the regiment's entire pre-war complement of officers, Lalor was one of only three accepted for overseas service with the 1st Battalion, although he had to accept a demotion in rank and sailed for England as a lieutenant.[5]

A 35-year-old Aspdin-area farmer in 1914, Lalor proved himself at the Second Battle of Ypres as machine gun officer for the 1st Canadian Infantry Brigade, receiving both the Military Cross and the French Legion of Honour. By the end of 1918, Lalor had risen to lieutenant-colonel commanding the 2nd Battalion, Canadian Machine Gun Corps.[6] Retaining an interest in the local militia following the war, Lalor was appointed commanding officer of the Northern Pioneers in the mid-1920s.

From 1927 to 1936, the Northern Pioneers took part in a series of brigade camps for summer training. The Northern Pioneers alternated in hosting or visiting with the Simcoe Regiment, the Grey Regiment, and the Algonquin Regiment from northern Ontario. During the annual camps, Pegahmagabow must have been in his glory, instructing and parading during the excursions to such places as New Liskeard, Orillia, Huntsville, Owen Sound and Penetanguishene.

In a 2003 interview, 88-year-old Roy O'Halloran, who would experience combat first-hand as a Second World War infantry lieutenant, and later was mayor of Parry Sound, recalled Pegah-magabow: "Peggy was a good guy. He was a sergeant-major in 'A' company of the Northern Pioneers and we used to go to camp together every year for a couple of weeks. New Liskeard was one of the first camps I went to in 1930 and we were billeted near the old racetrack grounds. Peggy used to come around and show us how to clean up and keep from getting soaked in the tents, you know, after a heavy rainstorm. He'd been around quite a bit. He was more like a father type to me. At that stage I was only 16 and I considered him a real fine old man. Of course, he was from the First World War and I was just a young fellow. I thought the world of Peggy. He was good to me. And he had the respect, I think, of most of the company."[7]

By 1935, Depression-era economics necessitated huge cutbacks in military spending and the militia was considered the least essen-

Lt.-Col. William J.A. Lalor, MC (right), commanded the 23rd Northern
Pioneers until June 1936. (*Mrs. Doug Sproat*)

tial section of Canada's military establishment. Units were given
a year to decide whether to merge with a nearby unit of a similar
type such as infantry or artillery, to convert to another arm of
the services under Ottawa's direction, or to disband. In December
1936, the Northern Pioneers amalgamated with "B", "C", and "D"
companies of the Algonquin Regiment, with the new regimental
headquarters at North Bay.

Percy Ball, who was 75 when interviewed by John Macfie in 1989,
also remembered Pegahmagabow: "On the second-last day before
we disbanded they sent a brigadier down from Ottawa, all gold
and red, and he went up and down [inspecting the men]. When he
came to Peggy he stopped and had quite a talk. So us young bug-

gers were kind of curious, and when we got around Peggy when it was over we said, 'What were you talking about, Peggy?' I can see the grin on his face yet. He said, 'Now boys, it was nothing. He just asked me how he was doing, and I just said, "Just carry on, brigadier, just carry on."' A big twinkle in his eye. We knew damn well that wasn't what they talked about. Peggy was pretty well known among military people."[8]

Pegahmagabow's active militia service seems to have ended with his unit's amalgamation with the Algonquin Regiment, but it concluded on a high note, for in the fall of 1936 the Parry Sound boys returned from the annual training camp at Penetanguishene with the regimental cup for shooting. Apparently, Pegahmagabow had taught his peacetime volunteers well. The old soldier himself was recognized on the parade grounds as the best-turned-out NCO.[9]

Pegahmagabow's return to uniform did not solve his problems, however. Despite the medical attention he had received on his return home from the war, Pegahmagabow's health continued to be a concern. Money—or the lack of it—also remained a problem. And both of these contributed to difficulties between him and his wife and growing family.

Early in 1930, Parry Sound practitioner Dr. Kenneth Andrew Denholm, who worked part time for Indian Affairs seeing to the medical needs of Indians under Daly's jurisdiction, sent Pegahmagabow to the Christie Street Hospital in Toronto for a thorough examination, hoping he might qualify for a pension. Dr. Denholm, who had served overseas as a captain in the Canadian Army Medical Corps, told the hospital that Pegahmagabow suffered from weak spells, shortness of breath, cough, and pain in the side and back.

As Duncan Pegahmagabow later recalled, "He could never sleep laying down because of the condition of his lungs, he would choke. He sat up so there was always a chair, an easy chair, by the stove. Of course, we didn't have electric heat, so the stove was always kept going."[10]

The doctor advised that his heart was irritable, and that his pulse rose quickly and stayed up. He also stated Pegahmagabow had hallucinations of being shot and "if he is in contact with curious people his mind goes blank, and he must be alone. These are probably symptoms of some neurosis of traumatic origin."[11]

While First World War doctors could adequately repair simple bullet wounds, psychiatry was still in its infancy. They knew little about the manifestations that could result from shell shock and head injuries. Pegahmagabow's medical records make several references to him being buried by shellfire and rescued by his fellow soldiers, bleeding from his ears on at least one occasion. Pegahmagabow himself wrote to the pension commission:

At last part of the war my head did not work with me so well, I just simply go out of my mind, but not as a crazy man as the boys tell me. I go about front same as usual in daytime ... Anyway, as gossip make it, I am supposed to be half crazy now...[12]

Daughter Marie Anderson remembers her mother telling her that married life with Francis was very difficult for her at first. "She said when I first married your dad I was very scared of him because any little bang he'd jump up. His nerves were on edge, I guess. And she said she couldn't stand it."[13] Both Anderson and her sister-in-law Priscilla Pegahmagabow also recall that he would always grab his hat and coat and disappear into the bush alone during thunderstorms. They surmise thunder brought back terrible memories of artillery barrages, and he did not want anyone, even his family, to see that he was afraid.[14]

Anderson related anecdotes she heard from her mother as a child that indicate that although her father was usually quiet and peaceful, he may have been deeply troubled. One particular story involved the death of a sibling, Leo James Pegahmagabow, on June 30, 1925. A relative who dabbled in witchcraft told Francis that he had not fathered the three-month-old child. As Anderson told it: "He got up to leave. She said this baby doesn't belong to you. He's got blue eyes. Sure enough when my dad walked in the house my mother said the first place he went was for the baby. He picked up the baby in the cradle and took the baby to the light. Sure enough the baby's eyes were light. He took this baby and threw the baby in the crib. This baby's not mine. It was this aunt that put that in his head. My mother didn't even have a chance to tell him that babies' eyes change."[15]

A former neighbour, 71-year-old Levi Nanibush, recalled in 1991 that he witnessed numerous arguments between Pegahmagabow and his father, Jonas, while Levi was growing up. He said sometimes Pegahmagabow would get into his "ugly mode" and "come raise hell in our house."[16] Usually, the arguments were rooted in Pegahmagabow's belief that Jonas, a descendent of Potawatomis from Michigan who had been living on Parry Island since 1877, did not belong there. "Trouble in his mind, I guess," Nanibush said.

And yet, Nanibush was also quick to point out Pegahmagabow's quieter and gentler side. As a teenager, he often worked for the former chief, cutting wood for cottagers. "And he paid me there one time…before the Second World War, he gave me $10," Nanibush recalled. "I thought I was rich. That was during the Depression. Ten dollars was a lot of money."

After Nanibush went into the Royal Canadian Artillery in 1942, Pegahmagabow corresponded with the young soldier throughout his service in North Africa and Europe. "He used to tell me what was happening. About the people I knew. If someone died, of course, he'd let me know."

Both Duncan and his sister Marie each spoke of a happy childhood. "You know, you talk about a soldier, you think of a hard person, but he wasn't," Duncan said. "He was a good man. And my mother never did any work except for handicrafts. My father did the laundry. He did the floors."[17]

"Him and my mother were a pretty good team together," Marie said. "She was a very good craft person. Every time she sold her crafts, she put the money aside. When there would come a time he had to go [somewhere], she'd get her money and put it there for him. He'd make sure she had everything in the house before he left. She helped him quite a bit. She helped him a lot."[18]

Marie also recalled that her father had quite a sense of humour and played lots of tricks on his boys. One time, she said, her father had some fun at the expense of son Robert, who was always slow rising from his bed in the morning and then rushed to get out of the house for his job as a mechanic. One morning, Robert was in such a hurry to get out the door he didn't notice that the can marked Brylcreem actually contained syrup. "He's over there grooming himself, had his Brylcreem open, slapping it on. Pick up his cap and walk outside. I could hear my brother: 'Shit! Who did this?' Hear the can flying in the garbage. My dad come back. Nobody say a word. Big smile on his face."[19]

Interestingly, esteemed anthropologist Diamond Jenness, who spent seven weeks on Parry Island during the summer of 1929 speaking at length with band members for his book *The Ojibwa Indians of Parry Island: Their Social and Religious Life*, didn't seem to question Pegahmagabow's mental abilities. Jenness based many of his conclusions on stories related to him by Pegahmagabow, whom he found to be "profoundly meditative." He wrote:

Being of profoundly meditative temperament, he began to write down the lore of his people, but later lost the notebooks in which he had jotted down their customs and traditions. He was elected chief of the Parry Island Indians after he returned from the war and held the position for two years when he stirred up some opposition by urging the old men and women to narrate in the council house the earlier customs of the people. Although comparatively young, and more travelled than most of the Indians, he was more saturated with their former outlook on life than the majority and more capable of interpreting the old beliefs. Occasionally his interpretations may have been a little more advanced than the average

Indian would have given, yet they were a logical development of the lay beliefs such as were possible to any philosophically minded Ojibwa before the coming of Europeans.[20]

Pegahmagabow's notions of the supernatural, witchcraft and sorcery were scoffed at by non-believers, but they were very real to the veteran and Jenness, as well, took his statements very seriously, although he was the only one of the anthropologist's five Parry Island informants to express a concern about being attacked by sorcery. Later in life, Pegahmagabow would move his family out of their home because he was convinced it was haunted and into a rented dwelling elsewhere on the reserve. "Just why he left his own home I could never properly understand, but there is some silly tale of ghosts," wrote the Indian agent who succeeded Daly. Although the band council authorized a $200 loan for Pegahmagabow to purchase the second house from Harry Medwayosh, the Indian agent advised his superiors against this.[21]

Jenness reported Pegahmagabow's comments on the sorcery:

Last spring an owl prowled around my house just at the time my baby was born. I could not kill any game, and became seriously ill, while my family was starving. Neighbours advised me to shoot the owl, but I knew that even if I hit it the bird would simply disappear and my gun would be quite useless afterwards. Then one of my friends who had been tapping some maple trees said to me "I'll see if I can help you when I get home." No sooner had he reached his home when I began to kill game again and to catch all the fish I needed. So I know some medé or sorcerer had a grudge against me and sent this owl to molest me.[22]

Mrs. John Manatuwaba is herself a witch. Last winter my wife was very ill, and Jim Nanibush gave me herbal medicine to sprinkle over the walls, doors, and windows of my house four days in succession to make the witchcraft recoil on the sorcerer's own head. A fortnight later Mrs. Manatuwaba's niece died, and soon after-

wards her grandchild. Her own daughter-in-law then reproached
her, saying "You have been trying to bewitch other people and your
sorcery has recoiled on your own family."[23]

In April 1930, the Board of Pension Commissioners awarded
Pegahmagabow a disability pension for bronchitis and emphy-
sema, which it found to be attributable to his military service.[24]
The board made the award retroactive to his discharge, and a sum
of $959.50 was deposited into the Bank of Nova Scotia in Parry
Sound. The bank's manager, George Lichty Ziegler, and Indian
agent Daly became trustees of the money.

A further $6.15 a month was paid into the account to help sup-
port Pegahmagabow, his wife, and their three children, William
Joseph, Michael Archibald, and Robert Henry.[25] The payments
would have been more had Pegahmagabow not opted for a Returned
Soldiers Insurance Policy with monthly premiums of $8.15.

While the pension was intended only to help Pegahmagabow
better the circumstances of his family, Pegahmagabow resented
the fact that Daly was allowed to administer the money and viewed
it as just one more aspect of his life that the Department of Indian
Affairs had control over. He claimed Daly used the money as a way
to restrain his actions and complaints against the department.

"He get it tied up in the bank so I could only get it with his
approval," Pegahmagabow wrote. "Then when I call for it he
expect me to get down on my knees for it and get sore before he
would write me out a cheque."[26]

That Daly fully expected Pegahmagabow to be indebted to him
is shown by Daly's furious reaction at a Parry Sound town council
meeting upon learning that Pegahmagabow and three others had
sent a letter to Ottawa objecting to the initial plan to operate a
ferry between Bob's Point in Parry Sound and Deepwater Point
on Parry Island, a scheme that Daly endorsed personally.

"In reply [Daly] stated that he did not care a snap of his fingers
for the letter. He said he was responsible for securing a pension

for one of the writers of that letter and this was his method of saying thank you. Mr. Daly said he would do his duty as he sees fit and that such a letter would not change his stand in any way."[27] Daly commented to Indian Affairs that Pegahmagabow was "the most ungrateful piece of humanity that I have ever run across" and that he was contemplating approaching the Pension Commission to have Pegahmagabow "examined mentally."[28]

Pegahmagabow's feelings of dependence and humiliation at having to go to Daly for his pension money came to be shared by dozens more. After the economic collapse that began around 1930, Daly came to enjoy maximum power and influence as scores of unemployed natives who came begging for assistance had no choice but to submit to his authority. Most of the men found themselves building and repairing roads in exchange for relief, but Daly exploited the opportunity to dispatch those he personally disliked to distant locations to perform arduous and unpleasant labour. He was ruthless in seeing that those whom he perceived as malingerers were made to work.[29] In March 1935, Daly instructed the native foreman:

> *Isaac Rice was here at this office the other day stating that he was sick (I never saw him looking better) and he had substituted his nephew. While this is all right in the case of severe sickness, or satisfactory explanation to me, I do not think that Isaac Rice is very sick and he can go ahead with his work. Get after Rice to see that he attends to his work.*[30]

Isaac Rice, who had been wounded in the right arm in the assault on Passchendaele in 1917, was supporting a wife and six children on an annual income of just over $300, including a meagre military pension, before Daly began paying him $10 a month in relief payments.[31] In May 1936, the Canadian National Railways general agent at Depot Harbour informed Rice that he had been instructed not to give him any further employment because of his physical unfitness, but Daly knew more than two years earlier that he was "in very poor health" and "not able to keep himself."[32]

During the Depression years, treaty Indians were not eligible for the same assistance as other veterans under the War Veterans' Allowance Act. It was decided in the spring of 1932 that Indian veterans on reserves in need of help were to be treated like other Indians on reserves rather than as veterans, and only enfranchised Indians not living on reserves were entitled to the same benefits as white veterans. The living allowance of $40 a month for a single and $70 for a married veteran accorded by the War Veterans' Allowance Act was far more generous than any assistance provided by Indian Affairs. Finally, in 1938, J.C.G. Herwig of the Canadian Legion's Dominion Command demanded and received equal treatment for Indian veterans on reserves.[33]

Despite an obvious shortage of money, Pegahmagabow was determined that his two eldest sons would have better educational opportunities than he had. William and Michael were sent to St. Vincent's Orphanage in Peterborough in 1931, where they were raised and educated by the Sisters of St. Joseph, along with some forty other boys. "I have two boys at school, they must be well dress[ed] ... or they will be sent home with broken spirit," he wrote Brigadier-General Hill, who had resigned two months earlier as commissioner of the New Brunswick Provincial Police. "I want to encourage the boys as much as I can."[34]

Percy Ball, who remembers Pegahmagabow as "the most honourable man I ever met," fondly recalls an anecdote from this period of Pegahmagabow's life that shows that regardless of how little money the former soldier may have had in his pocket, he always remembered and repaid his debts. "I lied abut my age when I was 17, and got to a Northern Pioneers militia camp in Penetang. You had to be 18, and I would be 18 in December, so I didn't lie too much. Anyway, Francis Pegahmagabow was there with us at Penetang, and near the end of the two-week camp several of us went into Penetang. In the course of the evening, Peggy asked if

Some members of the Parry Island band in 1939. Isaac Rice is in the back row, second from right. In the front row (from left) are Albert J. King, Elijah Tabobondung, Willie W. King, and band constable Stephen Partridge. (*David L. Thomas Collection / Wasauksing First Nation, Tray 1-48*)

he could borrow fifty cents from me. I don't know how I happened to have a spare fifty cents, but I cheerfully gave it to him. The years went by, and in 1939 when I was working at Kirkland Lake I came down for my sister's wedding, and while here I went into what we called 'Parry Hoot' for an evening. While standing on Beatty's Corner a man walked up to me and said he owed me fifty cents, and tried to hand it to me. I said, 'I'm sorry, I think you've made a mistake.' He said, 'Oh no, I haven't. You loaned me fifty cents in Penetang one night.' All those years he never seen me, and I'm quite sure he didn't even know my name, but he remembered my looks, be they good or bad. Now that's an honest man."[35]

Isaac Rice poses with tourists during the 1930s.
(David L. Thomas Collection / Wasauksing First Nation, Tray 4-28)

Pegahmagabow's financial situation improved a little after a medical examination at the Christie Street Hospital in February 1940, when the Department of Pensions and National Health decided to adjust his pensionable disability to twenty per cent or $26 per month (minus $15 for the Returned Soldiers Insurance Policy).[36] The decision came eleven days before the birth of Pegahmagabow's youngest child, Marion Anastasia (Marie), which increased the size of the family to six children, including four-year-old Duncan Angus and six-year-old Florance May.

It is ironic that while it was war that first brought Pegahmagabow to prominence as a Canadian hero, it took another world

Eva Pegahmagabow (left) and Isaac Rice's wife, Rosie.
(David L. Thomas Collection / Wasauksing First Nation, Tray 1-44)

conflict to bring him financial relief. After Canada declared war on Germany in 1939, the relatively small Canadian Industries Limited (CIL) plant at Nobel, north of Parry Sound, converted to the wartime production of military explosives, as it had done during the First World War. At the request of the Canadian government, it also set up a subsidiary company in the same area known as Defence Industries Limited (DIL) for the production of trinitrotoluol (TNT) and cordite. The company, which was built, operated, and managed by CIL, employed some 4,100 workers between 1940 and the spring of 1944.

In 1941, Pegahmagabow became a guard at the DIL plant, no

doubt due to his superior service record in the previous war. Three-quarters of the plant guards were veterans, thus freeing up younger men for military service overseas. With periodic absences, Pegahmagabow worked at DIL until receiving his seven-day layoff notice on June 7, 1945.[37]

An August 1943 article in the company's internal newspaper, *Nobel News*, recounted Pegahmagabow's wartime exploits, at one point quoting verbatim from Indian Affairs' 1919 annual report:

In addition to the 378 enemies disposed of by sniping it is said that he also accounted for 20 by bayonet, eight by clubbing and two by strangulation. This proves that what we call commando tactics are an old story to the Indians...

The Indians in warfare have always had unbounded courage, intelligence, initiative and an amazing stamina and have readily adapted themselves to discipline. In daring and intrepidity they were second to none. It was not long before Francis's officers found out that he had that instinct, or sagacity, inherited from a long line of forest fighters, of finding his way around in the dark by stealth and that he could penetrate the enemy's lines and return safely almost at will.[38]

While Pegahmagabow was working for the war effort at Nobel and permitted his employer to intimidate other workers with his impressive war record, it is clear he felt natives should not be compelled to fight overseas. He was acutely aware that an order-in-council (PC 111), passed January 17, 1918, had amended the Military Service Act of 1917 to allow natives to apply for exemption from service as combatants, through their respective Indian agents, provided they were registered at the post office. There was also a provision for natives to apply for exemption from service altogether.

During the Second World War the National Resources Mobilization Act, passed on June 20, 1941, called for the registration of

Guards, many of them First World War veterans, pose in front of the gatehouse at Defence Industries Limited in Nobel. Francis Pegahmagabow stands in the third row, far right.

all men and women who had reached 16 years of age. Although military service overseas was to be voluntary, all young men were required to undergo thirty days military training, and those not going overseas were compelled to serve within the western hemisphere for the duration of the war. The Department of Justice ruled that Indians could not be excused from this form of military service.[39]

One native who Pegahmagabow tried repeatedly to get out of the military on behalf of his parents was Shawanaga band member Charles Nanibush, an Algonquin Regiment recruit. "It is observed that you are a distinguished soldier of the Great War and you are therefore fully conversant with the duties of a soldier in His Majesty's Forces," Lieutenant-Colonel J.P. Richards wrote back to Pegahmagabow in August 1941. "Spr. Nanibush seems to be quite happy here and we are firmly of the opinion that he will be an excellent soldier when he has completed his training."[40] Tragically, Lance-Corporal Charles Nanibush was killed in action in March 1945 at age 25, shortly before the war in Europe ended.

In October 1941, Pegahmagabow wrote directly to Prime Minister Mackenzie King about the registration for military service of his "young fellow Indians."[41] The Prime Minister's Office directed the letter to Indian Affairs, who in turn gave it to Samuel Devlin, the new Indian agent at Parry Sound, with instructions to advise Pegahmagabow that "in future all communications of the kind should be forwarded through your office"—where they could be squelched before they went any further.

Neither of Pegahmagabow's two eldest sons were particularly enthusiastic about serving in the military, especially William, who was to be called up in 1941 at age 21. After Pegahmagabow wrote to the Department of National War Services indicating that the youth contributed significantly to the impoverished household, his attestation and training was postponed until April 1943.[42]

Six months after his army induction, William began scheming to obtain a release on the grounds of poor health, a plot that eventually earned him a discharge from the Royal Canadian Army Service Corps. "I'm still trying something that's going to make me dam sick, but I am trying it once," William confided in an October 1943 letter to his father from Red Deer, Alberta. "It's something the army doctors won't get wise to and there is nothing they can do about it either."[43]

Whatever his plan, it obviously worked. "I am getting a discharge from here out of the army," William gleefully wrote his younger brother Michael in April 1944, a month before his discharge. "I had a reboard here about a week ago and the doctors pretty near took me apart and they asked me how the hell I got in the army in the first place."[44]

While working as a munitions packer at DIL, 20-year-old Michael enlisted voluntarily in April 1942 to avoid being called up, but then changed his mind while undergoing training in Kitchener, Ontario. He wrote to Indian Affairs trying to get an exemption from the Military Service Act under the 1918 amendment:

> *I know it is going to be very hard this winter and my dad is not very well, his wound [from] last war on his leg is going bad. So will you please let me to go back home? I would like to go back to my job at DIL. I help the war effort better there.*[45]

Samuel Devlin informed Indian Affairs that he could not think of any valid reason why Michael should be excused from his duty, going on to write that he was, in fact, Absent Without Leave (AWL) and the military authorities were actively searching for him.[46] Michael finally received a discharge on compassionate grounds in January 1944.[47]

CHAPTER 5

The Indian Activist

IN JANUARY 1998, Canadian Indian Affairs minister Jane Stewart offered a landmark statement of reconciliation to the country's 1.3 million Indian, Inuit, and Métis peoples for racist attitudes and government policies aimed at suppressing their languages and cultures. She pledged that henceforth the federal government would work "government-to-government, nation-to-nation" with Canada's aboriginals.[1]

On behalf of the government, Stewart promised $350 million over four years for a healing fund to help communities cope with the devastating effects of the residential school system. There was also a commitment to provide more money for native housing and to upgrade water and sewage facilities; to invest in head-start programs for aboriginal children and to preserve aboriginal languages; and to provide stable and predictable transfer payments to aboriginal governments and institutions.[2]

Journalists eager to explain these developments stated that they were the result of the 440 recommendations contained in the $58-

FACING PAGE Francis Pegahmagabow wearing his medals and decorations in June 1945. He was in Ottawa attending the conference where the National Indian Government was formed under the leadership of Supreme Chief James Fox, but with Jules Sioui holding the real power as executive secretary. *(Canadian Museum of Civilization, 95292)*

million report of the Royal Commission on Aboriginal Peoples, formed following the Oka confrontation. Most also attributed the government's promises to the August 1997 election of Phil Fontaine as leader of the Assembly of First Nations, which represents about 500,000 status Indians in Canada.

In truth, impatience by the town of Oka to enlarge a nine-hole golf course in 1990 brought to a boil a land controversy involving the Kanesatake people that had been simmering for nearly a century. And the desire by Canada's aboriginal peoples to be treated as a nation isn't new. In 1923, Deskaheh, Cayuga Chief Levi General, travelled to Geneva, Switzerland, with a petition for self-government that explained the independence and sovereignty of the Six Nations Confederacy, but the League of Nations refused to hear it.[3] The Confederacy petitioned the United Nations for membership in 1952.[4]

The Canadian government's admission of regret for its previous policies came as a consequence of more than half a century of protest and opposition by several generations of aboriginal leaders. Starting with Frederick O. Loft's League of Indians in the 1920s, they have won change through one small victory at a time.

Indeed, the Second World War was a catalyst that convinced native leaders of the immediate need for a loud unified voice representing bands across Canada. They were concerned about the National Resources Mobilization Act and the possibility that Indian conscripts would be sent overseas against their will, especially after the majority of Canadians voted to release the government from its pledge not to extend conscription to overseas service in a national plebiscite, held in April 1942.

There was also the long-standing complaint that natives were required to pay income taxes on money earned off the reserves, even though they did not have the full benefits of Canadian citizenship and could not vote. Provincial government domination of fishing, hunting, and trapping—upon which many natives depended for their livelihood—was another sore point.

In June 1943, Andrew Paull, a 51-year-old Squamish from North Vancouver who had been active in the Allied Tribes of British Columbia, met at Caughnawaga, Quebec with a handful of representatives from the native communities at Lorette, Kanesatake, and Caughnawaga. Together they launched a plan to form the Brotherhood of Canadian Indians. While the committee members chose Paull as president, the burden of organizing a founding convention of native leaders from across Canada fell on Lorette representative Jules Sioui, whom they appointed secretary.

Dubbing himself Chief of the Committee for the Protection of Indian Rights, the 37-year-old Sioui immediately began sending letters to every Indian band across Canada inviting them to send delegates to a national conference in Ottawa in October. Sioui was well known to Indian Affairs as a "chronic troublemaker and agitator" who was under investigation by the RCMP for counselling Indians not to comply with national registration and military service requirements.[5]

The reaction from Indian Affairs was swift, as it advised the various bands across Canada, through their agents, that Sioui was not an actual chief and had, in fact, been defeated by another candidate 39–73, when he contested the position in the 1938 council elections of the Jeaune Lorette band. The agents were also advised that while the department had no power to prevent delegates from attending the convention, they would be doing so at their own expense, and "in the opinion of the department there is no way in which their interests can be helped by attendance at the meeting or participating in the activities of Mr. Sioui or the organization he represents."[6]

Re-elected chief of the Parry Island band in January 1942, almost two decades after being forced from the office, Francis Pegahmagabow received Sioui's invitation with excitement and turned a deaf ear to his agent's entreaties that he not attend the Ottawa convention. Once a valiant soldier, who in 1919 had eagerly remarked to a *Toronto Evening Telegram* reporter that he would immediately go to war again if called upon to do so, Pegahmagabow had become cynical, and distrusted Indian Affairs and its local agents, whom he felt had systematically blocked every opportunity he'd had to get ahead in life.

As reserve lands could not be mortgaged or sold, the only way for an Indian to get together a sizable amount of money was to borrow it from band funds. However, even if the band council agreed to make a loan, the resolution had to be approved by Indian Affairs.

On five different occasions—October 1920, April 1921, August 1922, December 1922, and March 1939—the Parry Island council passed resolutions granting loans to Pegahmagabow to purchase a team of horses to use in clearing his land, and in each case Indian Affairs vetoed its decision. Seething with anger after being denied for the fifth time, Pegahmagabow complained to Parry Sound MP Arthur Slaght, and although this letter appears not to have survived, Slaght's written response to Daly clearly reflects how worked up the veteran must have been:

> It would appear to me that this man must be a troublemaker when he uses language of this kind, and I am advising you, in confidence, so that you may put this letter away in an appropriate file. Barking dogs seldom bite, but if this man should try to make any trouble later on, I am filing his letter away here, under his name in my misc. file, so that he could be properly punished, and it could be established that he had put forward threats of violence.[7]

Pegahmagabow's animosity for Indian Affairs was intensified by a strong dislike for Samuel Devlin, a former private in the 4th Division Ammunition Column, a wartime subordinate who now exercised total bureaucratic control over his life by virtue of the Indian Act. It probably would have added to Pegahmagabow's disenchantment had he known that the Irish-born Devlin spent only five months in France in 1917 before a kick from a horse got him

Samuel Devlin, Indian agent at Parry Sound April 1939 to July 1950.
(Royal Canadian Legion, Pioneer Branch 117)

invalided to hospital in England, where he served out the rest of the war in relative safety with the Canadian Forestry Corps. Prior to his appointment as Indian agent in April 1939, Devlin worked at Pakesley (forty miles north of Parry Sound) as yard foreman for the Milwaukee-based Schroeder Mills and Lumber Company.[8]

Pegahmagabow made his opinion of Devlin clear:

I have seen Indians has nothing to eat in their place. Sam Devlin just laugh at them saying "What do you think, I am Santa Claus?". He give rations only to the ones he like, and he will not speak a

word to get work for an Indian. He give us no protection. We go to
tell him the white people trespassing on our reserve he just laugh at
us. He would say: "Why not shoot them with an arrow?" He is a
man naturally hate an Indian.[9]

In total, some fifty-six delegates from fourteen bands, including Pegahmagabow, attended the conference in the convention
theatre of Ottawa's Victoria Museum while Indian Affairs tried
to downplay it to newspaper reporters as being "unauthorized"
and having "no official status." Department officials insisted they
had no idea why the Indians were there, even when the delegates
headed for Parliament Hill attempting to present a petition to the
prime minister.[10]

Many delegates stretched their finances to the absolute limit
to attend the conference, including Pegahmagabow and Shawanaga representatives Solomon J. Pawis and Henry K. Abetung,
who had no money to pay their bill at the Windsor Hotel. Indian
Affairs covered the $18 hotel bill, but the three men had to sign a
promissory note to indemnify the government out of their annual
interest payments.[11]

Even though Sioui became the obvious focus of Indian Affairs'
attempts to discredit the delegation in the newspapers, several
reporters wrote about the colourful Pegahmagabow, who donned
his service medals with his native regalia and appeared every bit
a true patriot and hero.[12] One scholar has since made particular
note of the article that appeared in the *Vancouver Sun*:

Having noted his extraordinary record, and that of his band in
the previous conflict, the story closed with a stunning revelation:
"Friday he dropped in on the Canadian Legion and bought the first
poppy of this year's campaign. Then the Legion discovered that it
was his last 50 cents." That such an obviously capable man with
strong claims on society's generosity, as both a war hero and a
legal ward of the state, could be brought so low revealed something

PROVINCE DE OF QUÉBEC
- CANADA -

SEP 14 1943

COMITÉ DE PROTECTION DES DROITS INDIENS
Quartiers généraux au Village Huron de Lorette

Grand chef,

La présente communication vous avise de la tenue, à Ottawa, le 19 octobre prochain, d'une grande convention des chefs de notre nation. Je dois réclamer la présence, à l'hôtel Windsor, de deux ou trois délégués pour chaque tribu indienne.

Les heures graves que nous vivons nous forcent à ébaucher et à préciser des projets de réformes sérieuses. Nous devrons établir celles-ci sans retard si nous voulons sauvegarder nos droits, et cela, dans un pays qui est bien le nôtre.

Une réponse affirmative de tous est urgente. Votre aide financière sera aussi bienvenue, car le coût de ces travaux de réorganisation nous sont très onéreux.

Sincèrement.

Head chief : —

This letter advises you that a general meeting of the chiefs of our Nation will take place in Ottawa, on the 19th day of October next. I do claim the presence, at Windsor Hotel, of two or three delegates from each one of our reserves.

The impact of these perilous moments compels us to draw-up serious reforms. We have to establish such reforms in order to put a betterment in the Indian situation, and this, without delay, if we want the maintenance of our rights in our proper country.

An urgent affirmative answer is requested. A financial help will be welcome as this rally and the works to be performed are very expensive and their cost rests rather heavily on our shoulders.

Sincerely,

JULES SIOUI,
chef exécutif du — C. P. — chief executive.
Case postale Loretteville P. O. B.,
Comté de Québec County.

The notice sent by Jules Sioui in 1943 to every Indian band across Canada, inviting them to send delegates to a national conference in Ottawa in October. Some 55 delegates, including Pegahmagabow, attended the conference in the convention theatre of the Victoria Museum. *(Duncan Pegahmagabow)*

profoundly wrong with the country. Though he was undoubtedly trying to make a poignant comment, it is not clear whether the journalist recognized what a devastating indictment this story was of Canada's handling of First World War veterans and more particularly of its treatment of the First Nations. Certainly many readers may have interpreted the story that way. However, the journalist did not go beyond the veiled criticism to clarify precisely what this anecdote symbolized.[13]

Having someone of Pegahmagabow's stature included in the native delegation lent a certain legitimacy to their cause in the

National Indian Government executive secretary Jules Sioui first proposed an Indian identification card at the June 1945 convention. *(Duncan Pegahmagabow)*

press, although Indian Affairs clearly viewed him with the same trepidation and distrust as it did Sioui. While serving a three-year term as band councillor from 1933 to 1936, Pegahmagabow, as well as Chief John Manitowaba and Councillor Walter Judge, had strongly opposed Daly's efforts to use Indian statute labour to repair the Parry Island roads, claiming that the work was being done exclusively for the benefit of the vehicle owners at Depot Harbour. Daly had earlier proposed the car owners each pay a voluntary fee of $5 to the band for driving on reserve property, but Indian Affairs eschewed Daly's conciliatory effort, rigidly proclaiming there was no provision in the Indian Act for such a fee. The situation reached a crisis point in January 1935 when Daly, expecting violence on the reserve, requested the presence of RCMP and OPP constables to oversee the work.[14]

In May 1941, the RCMP had interviewed Pegahmagabow after a 1st Battalion pal forwarded a letter Pegahmagabow had written warning that natives were planning a revolt against the government:

> *The government seems to be quite confident that an Indian is not worth a cent, nor a word, nor a person, and that only a very good war material. Tell the boys the red man of Canada is about to resign away from the government. I feel sorry for the people and my fellow veterans. Trouble will now be opened to do its dirty work ...*[15]

In March 1944, Pegahmagabow stirred the pot once again by writing to Prime Minister Mackenzie King, lamenting "time after time, tribes from all over Canada have made petty petitions that our grievances be brought about to justice, always ends up to nil and cause us big expense." He warned that natives were preparing a strong document to deal with the lack of action.[16]

A haughty Devlin assured his concerned superiors in Ottawa:

> *The chief appears to be even a little less coherent than usual in this communication, which is not really in his best vein. His complaints, which are received daily at this office, cover a multitude of matters, but as to pinning him down to anything definite, I find that is not possible. His complaints are usually generalizations on Indian rights and wrongs and when boiled down, do not really mean anything. It is my personal opinion that the man is a mental case.*[17]

In April, the Parry Island council passed a resolution, seemingly derived from an earlier petition by the Caughnawaga band, stating that it had lost faith in the federal government and wanted to deal directly with Malcolm McDonald, the British high commissioner in Ottawa. Pegahmagabow then sent a copy of the Bill of Native Rights in Canada to McDonald, who didn't know what to make of it.[18] Indian Affairs smoothed the incident over:

> ... this department is always prepared to give full attention to any complaints or grievances where there appears grounds for them, but it has not been possible to find any substantiation for those of Chief Pegahmagabow, although the correspondence with him has continued over a period of more than 20 years.[19]

Sioui sent out notices for a second conference of the Brotherhood of Canadian Indians to be held in Ottawa in June 1944, and Indian Affairs again tried to discourage the various bands across Canada from sending delegates. Acting director of Indian Affairs R.A. Hoey wrote in a memo to Indian agents:

> You may tell them, moreover, in the name of the Minister ... that it is their patriotic duty at this extremely critical period, to remain at home and do their utmost to assist in the war effort and to refrain from travelling across the country at the beck and call of any agitator or group of agitators. It is felt that the better and more representative Indians who are loyal and respectable members of the community would not wish to cause unnecessary annoyance to the government at a time when all attention and effort should be directed towards the great drive for victory ...[20]

Once again, Pegahmagabow ignored Devlin's pleadings that he not go to Ottawa, turning his back on the local agent as natives from coast to coast apparently did for the first time. Whereas fifty-six delegates from six provinces had attended the conference the previous year, 200 delegates travelled to Ottawa in 1944, representing fifty bands from across Canada. There were also two Iroquois representatives from New York State.

At the conference, Sioui called for the dismissal of the Indian Affairs director, Dr. Harold W. McGill, who had recently recommended the eventual enfranchisement and integration of all Indians. Sioui also demanded to see the mines and resources minister, Thomas A. Crerar, whose ministry was ultimately responsible for Indian Affairs, but Crerar flatly refused to meet any delegation with Sioui in it, citing his criminal record, a 1938 conviction for defamatory libel.

According to a biography based on the reminiscences of John B. Tootoosis of Cut Knife, Saskatchewan, former president of the Union of Saskatchewan Indians, Crerar advised delegates that "such a person should not be in a leadership position for Indian people, that the leaders should be more respectable and dependable."[21] The ultimatum caused a deep division among the native leaders, just as Crerar hoped it would. And believing Crerar might be more willing to officially recognize the Brotherhood if Sioui were not holding office, some of the delegates persuaded him to publicly withdraw.

Crerar made a brief address to the delegates on the afternoon of June 7, before rushing off to a meeting of the war committee of cabinet to discuss the D-Day invasion of Europe. Tootoosis's biographers wrote that Crerar probably would not have done this if Indian Affairs had not been so anxious to get the abusive Sioui out of the picture.

Influenced by the two Iroquois delegates from New York State, the Brotherhood of Canadian Indians became more international in scope after Sioui's departure from the convention, and changed its name to the North American Indian Brotherhood. By acclamation, the delegates chose the significantly less radical Andy Paull as president, with Joseph Delisle from Caughnawaga becoming vice-president, and Henry Jackson of Christian Island, secretary.

As business agent for the Native Brotherhood of British Columbia, the educated Paull negotiated contracts with canneries and established prices for fish, but he also had an extensive background both as a native leader and as an intermediary with government. In 1927, he had gained national attention by presenting a massive land claim before a Special Committee of the Senate and House of Commons that represented almost every native band in B.C.[22]

Although Pegahmagabow lost his position as chief of the Parry Island band to Alfred Tabobondung in January 1945, he responded to yet another invitation from Sioui, who in 1944 had formed a rival organization, the League of North American Indian Nations, with Jim Horton of Manitou Rapids as the supreme chief and John B. Tootoosis as deputy chief. The group held a convention in June 1945 at Ottawa's YMCA facilities. Here the National Indian Government was formed, under the leadership of supreme chief James Fox of Melbourne, Ontario, but with Sioui holding the real power as executive secretary.[23]

Despite front-page coverage in the *Ottawa Evening Citizen*, Indian Affairs refused to have any contact with Sioui and his group during their convention, at which time Sioui told reporters that Indian Affairs held over $15 million in trust for Canada's Indians, the proceeds of oil royalties, land sales, and logging leases.[24] Sioui demanded that Indian Affairs turn this money over to the National Indian Government, as well as address the contentious issues of compulsory military service and income tax.

When Pegahmagabow, Sioui, Paull, and dozens of other native delegates headed to Ottawa in 1943 and 1944, officials at Indian Affairs refused to meet with them and had, in fact, done their very best to discourage them from attending. After the 1945 NIG convention by Sioui and his followers, Indian Affairs realized the situation had gone much too far and some concessions were necessary. They could not continue to ignore native protesters, especially now that the war was over.

There was rampant speculation among bureaucrats in the department that native leaders were consulting a lawyer and that a draft of a new Indian Act could be presented in the House of Commons as a private member's bill, without input from Indian Affairs. At the same time, representatives from the Six Nations were protesting at a United Nations conference in San Francisco that they had been guaranteed the status of an independent nation by the Treaty of Ghent, which ended the War of 1812. Attempting to diffuse an intense situation, Mines and Resources minister J. Alison Glen, deputy minister Dr. Charles Camsell, and R.A. Hoey, the newly appointed director of Indian Affairs, all attended the September 1945 convention of the North American Indian Brotherhood in Ottawa.[25]

In a speech to the NAIB delegates, J.A. Glen made a number of promises and concessions including a revision of the Indian Act; a $12-million program to construct Indian hospitals, day schools, nursing stations, and Indian homes; the assurance that native veterans would receive the same benefits as white veterans; the right to vote; and a pledge that Indians would henceforth be entitled to old age pensions.

In reference to Sioui's group, Mines and Resources Minister J.A. Glen stated at the September 1945 NAIB convention:

> *The organization represented here a few weeks ago did not make any representation to us. They did not officially recognize us and I want to assure you that we did not officially recognize them. So far as I know they were not in contact with us at any time during the course of their deliberations. Nobody in the government took their resolutions very seriously and the less said about them the better for everybody.*[26]

But Sioui and Fox did not just disappear, as Indian Affairs would have liked. In fact, within a week of Glen's address at the NAIB convention, Sioui and Fox were meeting with American native

Francis Pegahmagabow, photographed in June 1945 while in Ottawa.
(*Canadian Museum of Civilization, 95293*)

leaders at the YMCA in Detroit, Michigan. As a result of these discussions, the convention sent notices to both Prime Minister Mackenzie King and President Harry Truman that stated they accepted the provisions set out in the preamble of the United Nations charter, in relation to treaty obligations, and to which the Canadian and American governments subscribed. The notice to Prime Minister King read:

> *We therefore respectfully request you to recommend such legislation to the Parliament, as will be necessary to expedite full and complete financial settlement of all outstanding treaty obligations, now due to the Indians of the Dominion of Canada.*[27]

Pegahmagabow kept in contact with Sioui by mail, although the National Indian Government was never recognized by Indian Affairs in any official, or even unofficial, capacity. While he clearly believed that it was divisive and even counter-productive for there to be more than one national organization representing native interests, Sioui's National Indian Government represented the only real avenue for him to remain an active participant in the struggle for self-government. At one point Pegahmagabow wrote:

> *My friend Mr. Jules Sioui is a little too hasty, as he lead us too near the rapids before we land to portage down the river. I say the same to other Indian associations also in the same current of Indian question. We should be amalgamated into one body if we mean business at all, otherwise up to date we are just fooling around amongst ourselves by small bodies of associations trying to get wiser than the other Indian associations.*[28]

Pegahmagabow's exclusion from a convention held under the auspices of the NAIB on Parry Island in August 1946, and attended by twenty-four delegates from eleven bands across Ontario, probably pushed him into even an even closer association with Sioui and his group. Chaired by his old rival, Chief Alfred Tabobondung, the meeting resulted in the formation of the Union of Ontario Indians, an organization still active today. Chief Robert Marsden of Christian Island was elected president, Chief Tabobondung became vice-president, with Henry Jackson of Christian Island as secretary.[29]

In September 1946, Pegahmagabow attended the first parliament session of the National Indian Government at the YMCA in Detroit, and maintained an association with the organization over the next three years, although its influence and membership seems to have declined significantly during the period.[30] While representatives of the Indian Association of Alberta, the Manitoba Indian Association, the Native Brotherhood of British Columbia, the North American Indian Brotherhood, the Union of Ontario Indians, and the Union of Saskatchewan Indians gave testimony at a Special Joint Committee of the Senate at the House of Commons on the Indian Act in 1946–8, Sioui and his followers were not invited.[31]

Although not an eloquent writer by any standard, Pegahmagabow certainly was a prolific one, corresponding with natives and politicians across Ontario during the 1940s. Surviving letters show there was a hotbed of discontent among natives, involving a wide range of issues from unresolved land claims to curtailed fishing and trapping rights, and many sought guidance from Pegahmagabow.

Chief John Twain of the Temagami Indians, a delegate to the 1943 convention who had worked at the Nobel DIL plant during the war, wrote to Pegahmagabow seeking his advice on the band's struggle to obtain a legal reserve. The band had not been invited to, and consequently was not represented at the 1850 signing of the Robinson Huron Treaty at Sault Ste. Marie, when their ancestral hunting ground, covering parts of some 110 northeastern Ontario townships, was surrendered to the Crown by representatives from other bands.

After living in legal limbo for close to a century, the band wanted a reserve at Austin Bay, but the Ontario government would only agree to a portion of Bear Island in Lake Temagami, and refused to hand over that area's valuable timber resources, saying the Temagami Tourist Association would be furious if the Indians cut into the great scenic attraction. Chief Twain wrote:

> *The provincial government should be good and well satisfied for what they have already taken away from us Indians. They had sold trappers licence to white people and after the white trappers has cleaned out everything in the country, the Indians didn't have nothing to make a living…They have taken everything away from us and sell it to make tons of money for themselves and leave nothing for us. They don't even want us to have a reserve even though it looks pretty small.*[32]

Ed Kitchikeg of Webbwood, Ontario, asked if Pegahmagabow would act as an interpreter at the murder trial of his son-in-law, George Shawanda, of South Bay village on Manitoulin Island. According to the *Manitoulin Expositor*, 33-year-old Nora Shawanda, the mother of six children, died on the operating table at Mindemoya hospital following a savage beating.[33] Kitchikeg also wanted Pegahmagabow's help to hire a lawyer to represent him and his wife at the proceedings.[34]

Others wrote to Pegahmagabow to complain about the increasing interference with where and when they could hunt, trap, and fish after the provincial government announced in February 1940 that the 4,000 Indians in Northern Ontario would have to abide by the Game and Fisheries Act. As a result of a compromise agreement between the Ontario Department of Game and Fisheries and the federal Department of Indian Affairs, game wardens

The Ontario government announced in February 1940 that Indians in Northern Ontario would have to abide by the Game and Fisheries Act. (*Duncan Pegahmagabow*)

would no longer turn a blind eye to Indians hunting and fishing during the closed season.[35] The agreement abrogated the 1850 Robinson Huron Treaty that had guaranteed aboriginals "the full and free privilege to hunt over the territory now ceded by them, and to fish in the waters thereof, as they have heretofore been in the habit of doing..."

The Indians were even more alarmed when a Sudbury magistrate sentenced Fred Sinbert of Spanish River to 500 days in jail or a fine of $1,020 for possessing the pelts of beavers, otters, and a mink trapped on the reserve.[36] His lawyer had argued unsuccessfully that the Robinson Huron Treaty provided that there would be no interference with Indian fishing and hunting rights on the reserves.

In October 1946, shortly after returning from the first parliament of the NIG in Detroit, Pegahmagabow attended a secret meeting of native leaders at Biscotasing, Ontario, to discuss the growing problem. He later told a *Sudbury Daily Star* reporter that those at the meeting had protested the curtailment of their treaty rights and rigorously opposed the proposed changes to the Indian Act.

"Canada's 150,000 Indians are practically destitute," Pegahmagabow said. "They are dependent on the Indian Affairs Branch in Ottawa, which is composed of whites."[37] He said that Indians wanted an opportunity to live in their accustomed manner in accordance with the Robinson Huron Treaty provisions. "Indians are not receiving proper education. What schools there are do not fit the Indian to take his proper place in his own society, and certainly not in the society of white men."

Pegahmagabow's willingness to listen to the problems of his people obviously endeared him to them. At the annual NIG convention held at the Algonquin Hotel in Sault Ste. Marie, Ontario, in September 1949, Pegahmagabow was elected supreme chief for the coming year by his fellow delegates.

It was a tumultuous time when the government introduced legislation for a new Indian Act in 1950, but the minister of Citizenship and Culture, Walter Harris, withdrew Bill 267 after second reading in the face of strong protest from aboriginal organizations, who charged that it ignored most of the recommendations of the Special Joint Committee. Indeed, some Indians denounced it as an attempt to make Indian status so distasteful that Indians would voluntarily leave the reserves.[38] In his final hurrah in the media spotlight, Sioui staged a nationally publicized hunger strike for the return of Canada to the Indians in the spring of 1950.[39]

In September, some two dozen delegates from Ontario and Quebec, including Sioui, attended the annual NIG convention at Sudbury's Frontenac Hotel, where they unanimously rejected the provisions of Bill 267 and demanded recognition of an independ-

Francis Pegahmagabow and his wife, Eva (far right), at the first commu-
nion of their youngest daughter, Marion (Marie), in 1950. Others include
Beda, Lillian, and Harriette Judge, Phil Chechock, and Margo Missabae.
(Vince Chechock)

ent North American Indian Nation within the United Nations.[40] Delegates signed a strongly worded petition, no doubt inspired by one presented to the UN earlier that year protesting the attempts of Canada, the United States, and the State of New York to assume jurisdiction over the Six Nations Confederacy. They also re-elected Pegahmagabow to an unprecedented second term as supreme chief.

In an interview with a *Sudbury Daily Star* reporter, Pegahmagabow explained that when the Marquis de Vaudreuil, the governor of New France, signed the articles of capitulation in 1760, the Indian allies who had fought for the French were to be protected against reprisals, and they were to have liberty of religion and freedom to move as they wished. A key point in their present claim, Pegahmagabow said, was that they were recognized as allies of the French and not subjects of the French king; therefore, they were not a conquered people.

In 1850, when the Indians signed the Robinson Huron Treaty with William Benjamin Robinson, on behalf of the King, hunting and fishing rights were guaranteed on all lands ceded to the government of the time. "Now that has changed," Pegahmagabow told the reporter. "The original guarantees mean nothing. Indians are called on to buy hunting licences and are fined if they do not. We have petitioned the government for a hearing and we get nowhere. We must restore the Imperial treaty. Only the King can do that."[41]

Pegahmagabow insisted that only through the direct renewal of the original treaties with the Crown could Indians recover the rights taken from them by generations of white government. "The Indian Act must go. It has been changed and distorted so that now everything lies in the hands of one minister. There must be restitution for the timberlands which have been destroyed in spite of our stated rights to them. The Imperial treaty must be restored. It must be made with the King, because the [Canadian] government has shown that it cannot be trusted."

The National Indian Government's petition to the United Nations appears to have been pigeonholed, as was a 1952 petition for membership from the Six Nations Confederacy. While the UN and the earlier League of Nations ostensibly concerned themselves with the self-determination of nations, their concepts of nationhood were rigid and considerably different from those of the petitioners.

In 1951, the government successfully introduced Bill 79, a revised Indian Act that ended compulsory enfranchisement, whereby the federal government had the power to arbitrarily determine who could continue to be a legal Indian or who was fit for full citizenship status. Pegahmagabow had always opposed this practice, which originated with an Indian Act amendment in 1920.

The legislation also empowered the provinces to permit Indians to drink alcohol in bars and hotels, while curbing the power of Indian agents to veto band council resolutions and restrict democracy on reserves. It eliminated the bans on potlatch giveaway ceremonies of the coastal Indians of British Columbia and the Sun Dance of the Plains Indians, which Indian Affairs had viewed as barriers to Christianity and civilized conduct. But, perhaps most importantly, the 1951 revision of the Indian Act revoked the 1927 prohibition on soliciting funds to hire lawyers to fight claims unless the government approved.

Marie Anderson recalls that her father was still in fairly good health when his term as band chief ended in 1945. "And then he started as Indian advocate for all these different people. Used to come all the way over to house looking for him. And it was on these trips when he went away I noticed there was something strange about my dad every time he came back. He was weaker. He looked like he was sort of sickly. I could hear him choking in the middle of the night. I could hear him get up to go outside. Of course, we all got up to go outside during the night, but he'd be gone for a long, long time."[42]

The last known photographs of Francis Pegahmagabow were taken in Sept. 1950 during the National Indian Government convention, Sudbury.
(Duncan Pegahmagabow)

Francis Pegahmagabow died at St. Joseph's Hospital in Parry Sound on August 5, 1952, after suffering a heart attack while in town.[43] According to his son Duncan, the period of mourning at the Roman Catholic church on Parry Island was extended several times and eventually lasted more than three days, as people travelled from all over Ontario to pay their respects to an old warrior who had truly worn himself out in the service of his people.

As a member of the Brotherhood of Canadian Indians, and later the National Indian Government, he had been politically active during a period when progressive strides were made. Prior to the 1940s, the Department of Indian Affairs viewed Indian associations as an obstacle to its goal of assimilation because they fostered nativistic feelings in Indians. Inspired by trouble-making whites and dissident, unprogressive Indians, they interfered with the normal good administration of the department. By the 1960s, policy had so changed that Indian associations were encouraged as partners in the administration process.

Over the five decades since Francis Pegahmagabow's death, the family has always been extremely proud of their ancestor's accomplishments. Marie Anderson said her children frequently took their grandfather's medals from her dresser drawer without her permission for show-and-tell at school.[44] Her brother Duncan often wrote to the *Parry Sound North Star*. "The memories of my childhood are golden," he wrote. "My father was a tower of strength, a role model, and most of all a friend. Also, he was a very spiritual man but true to his church at the same time."[45]

Francis Pegahmagabow has also inspired descendents and others born long after his death. "He was our father, our grandfather, our great-grandfather, and our uncle," said Brian McInnis, a great-grandson, at the 2003 unveiling of the plaque on the Rotary and Algonquin Fitness Trail in Parry Sound. "It's also important for our community that we remember him, not just as the veteran of war or as a soldier, but also a man ... He believed very strongly in the vision of this country, and the potential of us to work together collectively to build something very beautiful and strong."[46]

Merle Pegahmagabow, a former negotiator for the Union of Ontario Indians who was a candidate for chief of Wasauksing in the 2009 band council election, said that he has been greatly influenced by membership in the Caribou clan, passed from father to son, and stories about his grandfather told to him by his grandmother. "It kind of bothered me that he never got any benefits from Veterans Affairs," he said. "I think my grandmother got a toilet installed in about 1960."[47]

Canadian Armed Forces Petty Officer First Class Rick Ten Eyck, a member of the Chippewas of Nawash, from Cape Croker First Nation on the Bruce Peninsula, convinced the family to allow the medals to be displayed at the 10th National Aboriginal Achievement Awards Gala at the National Arts Centre in Ottawa in March 2003. According to Anderson, this was the first step in the family's decision to donate the medals to the Canadian War Museum. Another First Nations soldier, Sergeant Kerry Ten Eyck of Princess Patricia's Canadian Light Infantry, proudly wrote in the *Parry Sound North Star* that Pegahmagabow and several other decorated aboriginal soldiers "were strong examples of those who placed a greater cause before their own lives."[48]

Afterword

AS A SCOUT, Francis Pegahmagabow moved silently, effortlessly across the battlefields of the First World War, gathering intelligence on enemy positions under cover of darkness without leaving a trace. As a sniper, he lay motionless and unseen by enemy observers, possibly for hours, waiting to take a lethal shot at a target behind the enemy lines. An expert at remaining undetected, Canada's most decorated First People's soldier didn't leave much of a trail at all for anyone trying to follow his exploits.

Pegahmagabow was one of only thirty-nine soldiers in the Canadian Expeditionary Force to be awarded the Military Medal and Two Bars for valour, yet he is not mentioned even once in the voluminous war diary of the 1st Battalion, the unit he served with for almost the entire duration of the war. On various occasions, the diary notes impromptu ceremonies where named soldiers were presented with the ribbons for various gallantry awards.[1] But never does Pegahmagabow's name appear. If not for the medals and the enduring tales of his prowess as a scout and sniper, it's as if he weren't there at all.

The lack of documentation on Pegahmagabow is not exceptional. First World War personnel files for Canadian soldiers are notoriously sketchy, and consist for the most part of detailed pay records, which the military at the time deemed to be of the utmost importance. The Holy Grail for information about Pegahmagabow's military service has always been the *Annual Report of the Department of Indian Affairs for the Year Ended March 31, 1919*, which was published in 1920. The brief account of Pegahmagabow's service in the war in this official government document was drawn almost entirely from a clipping from the August 28, 1919, *Toronto Evening Telegram*. The clipping had been placed in a file on Pegahmagabow's overseas duty at Indian Affairs.[2] Regrettably, the "official" summary is chock full of errors, which have been repeated over and over in books, newspapers, and elsewhere ever since. The summary reads:

> *About twenty Indians enlisted from the Parry Sound district. One of their number, Corporal Francis Pegahmagabow, won the Military Medal and two Bars. He enlisted in 1914 with the original 1st Battalion. He distinguished himself signally as a sniper and bears the extraordinary record of having killed 378 of the enemy. His Military Medal and two Bars were awarded for his distinguished conduct at Mount Sorrell [sic], Amiens, and Passchendaele. At Passchendaele, Corporal Pegahmagabow led his company through an engagement with a single casualty, and subsequently captured 300 Germans at Mount Sorrell [sic]. Corporal Pegahmagabow presented an address on behalf of his people to His Royal Highness the Prince of Wales upon the recent visit of the latter to Parry Sound.*[3]

I began researching the life of Francis Pegahmagabow in the late 1980s after reading a short article about him in the *Georgian Bay Beacon* by Parry Sound-area historian John Macfie, whose father, Roy, also served in the 1st Battalion during the First World War.[4] In 2003, Fox Meadow Creations published the results of my research as the biography *Pegahmagabow: Legendary Warrior, Forgotten Hero*, which is now out of print. I documented what I could to set the record straight, but the book continues to be overshadowed by misinformation.

In September 2003, journalist Peter Worthington wrote an extensive profile on Pegahmagabow that appeared in the *Toronto Sun, London Free Press*, and probably other Quebecor newspapers. It repeated a lot of the old claptrap, but also introduced a few new errors—such as that Pegahmagabow was decorated for heroism at Vimy Ridge and wounded twice.[5] Contacted by telephone, a rather testy Worthington refused to print a correction after I pointed out that Pegahmagabow was in hospital in England during the Battle of Vimy Ridge and was actually wounded only once, although he was hospitalized for pneumonia. The journalist Worthington termed these errors "irrelevant" and put me on the defensive by then accusing me of attacking a hero.

On another occasion, I was interviewed by *Toronto Star* reporter Joseph Hall, who was given a copy of *Pegahmagabow: Legendary Warrior, Forgotten Hero*. I said during the taped interview that Pegahmagabow won his Military Medal not for any particular action, but for carrying messages with great bravery between February 1915 and February 1916, through the actions at Ypres, Festubert, and Givenchy. The resulting article, which appeared in June 2006, stated that I had said Pegahmagabow was awarded his Military Medal for gallantry at Mount Sorrel.[6]

Government of Canada websites and Wikipedia haven't helped matters. A website for the Canadian Museum of Civilization insists, "There is no specific documentation on when Pegahmagabow won the Military Medal ... but evidence suggests he was awarded the Military Medal for his bravery at the June 1916 Battle of Mount Sorrel."[7] The improbability of this assertion should be readily apparent, given that the award was officially announced in the *London Gazette* on June 3, 1916, while the battle was still taking place.

Veterans Affairs Canada is not particularly interested either in learning about mistakes. When it published *Native Soldiers, Foreign Battlefields* in 1991, a soldier in a Library and Archives Canada photograph of 1st Battalion NCOs taken in January 1919 was iden-

1st Battalion NCOs in January 1919. Some sources claim the man at far left is Francis Pegahmagabow. *(Library and Archives Canada, PA-003831)*

tified as Francis Pegahmagabow—even though Pegahmagabow's personnel file states that he had been invalided to England in November 1918 and did not return to his unit.[8] Although I contacted the minister of Veterans Affairs and the book's author, Janice Summerby, about the apparent error in 1998, the photograph currently appears on a Veterans Affairs Canada website with one of the men identified as Pegahmagabow. The website also states "It is not known how Pegahmagabow earned the MM ..."[9]

In August 2007, University of Calgary professor Donna Coates delivered a refereed paper at the triennial conference of the Association for Commonwealth Literature and Language Studies, "Attention Must Be Paid: The Role of the Native Soldier in Joseph

Boyden's *Three Day Road*." In it she wrote that my biography of Pegahmagabow "slights his valor and superb marksmanship."[10] In defence, all I can say is that I made use of whatever documentation was available. I pointed out in a letter to the editor in a recently published issue of the *Globe and Mail* that while there can be no doubt that Pegahmagabow was a fearless soldier, it has also become apparent that the number of his confirmed hits as a sniper cannot be fully substantiated.[11] Although Métis sniper Henry Norwest, MM and bar, worked with a spotter, Private Oliver Payne, who confirmed all of Norwest's 115 hits, Pegahmagabow seems to have preferred to work alone and thus there probably were no Allied witnesses.

Pegahmagabow appears to have been interested in writing about his experiences in the First World War, and actually sought guidance from Brigadier-General F.W. Hill, the first commander of the 1st Battalion. Hill advised: "I think you should write your story yourself and in your own style. Your friends will help you to revise the copy and put what you have to say in suitable form and I will be happy to assist. But your own personal experiences are of value."[12] Unfortunately, Pegahmagabow simply did not have the ability to do this by himself and he seemingly never collaborated with anyone. His story could have become a best-seller like *A Rifleman Went to War* by Herbert W. McBride, an American who served as a sniper with the Canadian Expeditionary Force's 21st Battalion. One of the few written statements we have from Pegahmagabow about his skill with a rifle reads: "The best shot I ever made, about nine hundred yards away, long distance sniping. Man on horseback. Yes, I got him."[13]

Another obstacle that I encountered while researching the biography that became *Pegahmagabow: Legendary Warrior, Forgotten Hero* was the fact that most of his contemporaries and even his children were deceased. Duncan Pegahmagabow, the veteran's youngest son, spoke of his father from the perspective of a child who had idolized his dad, and as a result it was hard to reconcile his memories with the supposedly demented veteran portrayed in the Department of Indian Affairs records.

"He meant very much to me. He was not only a father but something I looked up to. I thought a lot about him. So much so that I never thought that he would die. I'm not kidding. That's what I thought. That he'd never die. So much I thought about him. So then the shock of his death, you can imagine what that was like for me," explained Duncan in a 1990 interview, when he was 53.[14]

The only other surviving child of Francis Pegahmagabow living on Wasauksing First Nation in 1990 was 49-year-old Marie Anderson, who at that time declined to be interviewed. When I tried to persuade her by telling her that I had already spoken with her brother, she replied, "Duncan remembers things differently than I do." An elder brother living in Cleveland, William Joseph, was very ill and died only a few months later.

There was also a strong reluctance of band elders on Wasauksing First Nation to talk about Francis Pegahmagabow. As a result, I was only able to record the memories of Levi Nanibush, 71, and James Edward Wheatley, 89, in interviews conducted in January 1991. Although Wheatley made repeated statements such as, "People didn't like him because he turned everything around," Nanibush was the first person I spoke to who referred to the veteran's "ugly mode."[15]

In writing *Pegahmagabow: Legendary Warrior, Forgotten Hero*, I struggled with the issue of Pegahmagabow's supposed dementia. Was he really crazy as the Indian agents Logan, Daly, and Devlin persistently wrote in their correspondence? And what was I to make of some of the musings in Pegahmagabow's own handwriting, such as a very odd diary entry for April 23, 1950? The entry reads:

Thirty-five years ago we suffered under the fumes of gas used in war of 1915 by Germans. I never want to see the agony of men in mass formation again. General [Sir Edwin] Alderson said Peg what can you do about this matter. I said try to change wind. He said alright go ahead. Yes the wind changes from east to west wind before the sun rise. Germans suffered just as heavy as we did. They were not prepared to take their own medicine ...[16]

Marie Anderson agreed to be interviewed in February 2005 when I was preparing a submission to the Historic Sites and Monuments Board of Canada (HSMBC) on behalf of Wasauksing First Nation and Parks Canada to have her father recognized as a Canadian of national importance. Through the many years after we had briefly spoken in 1990, Anderson had come to realize that her father had not received the recognition that he deserved. In 2002, she and her brother Duncan had written to the council of Wasauksing First Nation:

We have failed as a community to adequately recognize the distinguished service that this native son has provided to his homeland and the honour he has brought to the entire Anishnaabe Nation. It is our hope and desire that these many years of inaction may now be directed to honouring our father ...[17]

Anderson spoke candidly and never tried to evade a question. Some of her answers were surprising and totally unexpected. Her recollections confirmed for the first time that her father did in fact suffer from what we now know as post-traumatic stress syndrome, and he may have had dementia, which grew worse as he got older. Anderson told a story of her father dancing with the Queen of England at a party for soldiers: "He said he was in the corner with a bunch of his buddies and Queen Victoria come around and asked him to dance. He says I knew how to dance, but he said he was very shy. He said he got on the floor. He said he was dancing with the Queen. He said this was an honor for him...He said all these boys there and she picked him. He say he was scared, but didn't want her to know that."[18]

When asked the origin of her uncommon middle name, Anastasia, Anderson responded that this had been the name of her father's girlfriend in England. "My father had a girlfriend overseas. He didn't hold back from us. The girl there had a baby by him. He said he didn't want to go that far with that girl, but he said she was very pushy, I guess."[19]

"He did have some odd behaviour, and very quirky behaviour that scared the hell out of the kids from time to time," said current Anishinabek Nation Grand Council Chief John Beaucage, who previously served as chief of Wasauksing First Nation for eight years. In a 2009 interview, Beaucage, 56, said that he was a neighbour of Duncan Pegahmagabow and spent many hours sitting and talking with him. Beaucage recalled that whenever thunderstorms were approaching, Duncan's thoughts would tend to turn to his father because thunder apparently had caused him to act strangely. "I don't think that came out during the official discussion with Duncan I'm sure," Beaucage said, referring to my own 1990 interview with the veteran's son. "This was very unofficial."[20]

"He would sometimes put on his uniform and patrol the roads in the middle of the night to make sure the family and the community was safe, which I guess was fine, but it's very odd behaviour in peacetime," Beaucage said. And this odd behaviour is probably why elders did not wish to be interviewed about Francis Pegahmagabow, he suggested. "In a way it's a sort of a protection for the Pegahmagabow family, Francis and his children. I think they didn't want to tarnish the image of the war hero in any way, but yet the war hero was still a human being who had frailties."

The fact that Pegahmagabow had post-traumatic stress syndrome and behaved oddly at times does not in any way, however, rationalize or justify his postwar treatment—in fact, it makes it rather more despicable. Pegahmagabow returned to Canada unwilling to accept the status quo of reserve life and the overbearing authority of the local Indian agent. Unfortunately, his illness became a convenient excuse for the Department of Indian Affairs to dismiss his protests and complaints without properly investigating. It also probably frightened his own people and undermined his leadership. Members of the Parry Island band did not have any better understanding of head injuries or shell shock than the rest of Canadian society, said band elder Stewart King.[21]

And still Pegahmagabow soldiered on, determined to win a decisive victory.

Notes

Abbreviations

AO: Archives of Ontario
LAC: Library and Archives Canada
PP: Pegahmagabow papers
   (see note 17, Chapter 1)
PRO: Public Record Office
   (Kew, Richmond, Surrey, England)
VAC: Veterans Affairs Canada

Introduction

1 "Bitter legacy for brave native soldiers," *Toronto Star* Nov. 11, 1984: A23.

2 LAC, Record Group 10, vol. 7502, file 25022-5 (Reel C-14790), "Parry Sound Agency, Soldier Settlement, Francis Pegahmagabow, 1919–1935," Alexander Logan to Indian Affairs, Jan. 5, 1920. For more on the soldier settlement program administered by the Department of Indian Affairs see Robin Brownlie, "Work Hard and Be Grateful: Native Soldier Settlers in Ontario after the First World War" in Franca Iacovetta and Wendy Mitchinson, eds., *On the Case: Explorations in Social History* (University of Toronto Press, 1998) 181–203.

3 LAC, RG 10, Series B-3, vol. 7376, file 16022-17, "Perry Sound [sic], Band Loan, F Pegahmagabow," Alexander Logan to Indian Affairs, Aug. 17, 1922.

4 Fred Gaffin, *Forgotten Soldiers* (Penticton, B.C.: Theytus Books Ltd., 1985) 28, and Janice Summerby, *Native Soldiers, Foreign Battlefields* (Ottawa: Veterans Affairs Canada, 1993) 10–11.

5 Peter Kulchyski, "A Considerable Unrest: F.O. Loft and the League of Indians," *Native Studies Review*, 4.1–2 (1988) 95–117.

6 Michael Best, "Forgotten Heroes," *Toronto Star* Oct. 9, 1982: B5.

7 John Macfie, *Sons of the Pioneers* (Parry Sound: The Hay Press, 2001) 74; John Junck, "We should make an effort to honour a local war hero," *Parry Sound North Star* Apr. 11, 2000: 3.

8 Randy Boswell, "Sharpshooter honoured: Museum remembers most-decorated aboriginal soldier," *Vancouver Sun* Aug. 27, 2003: A7.

9 "First World War hero's artifacts go to war museum," *Ottawa Citizen* Aug. 28, 2003: A6.

10 Speech by Brigadier-General G.R. Thibault delivered June 6, 2006, at CFB Borden. Copy obtained by Master Cpl. W.L.R. McConnell, deployment clerk for 3rd Canadian Ranger Patrol Group.

11 A monument originally unveiled in September 2002 at the corner of Selkirk and Sgt. Prince Street in Winnipeg honours Prince as "Canada's most decorated aboriginal soldier." The monument has been relocated to the city's new Sgt. Prince Veterans Park, which was officially dedicated in June 2007. While *Legion Magazine* recently referred to Sgt. Prince as "Canada's most decorated aboriginal war veteran" ("Winnipeg Honours War Hero," Jan./Feb. 2003: 57), it now seems to have quietly amended itself by referring to Cpl. Pegahmagabow as "Canada's most decorated First Nations soldier" ("Aboriginal Veteran Honoured," July/Aug. 2006: 10–11).

12 Adrian Hayes, "Building to be named after most decorated Native soldier," *Parry Sound North Star* Apr. 12, 2006: 9.

13 Ibid.

14 Ibid.

15 Marie Anderson's comments to reporter Donna Smith, APTN National News Primetime, broadcast June 8, 2006.

16 Report 2005–6 written by Adrian Hayes submitted to the Historic Sites and Monuments Board of Canada in Apr. 2005 and considered by the Cultural Communities Committee during the June 2005 meeting. The committee and the full board have deferred a decision pending the receipt of more information. Specifically, they wished to know more about the history of national aboriginal organizations from the late 19th and early 20th centuries, and the leadership within these groups, so as to better understand the context in which to evaluate Pegahmagabow's achievements.

17 *The Kitchener Record*, July 13, 2007: D10.

18 Notes for an address to Assembly of First Nations Annual General Assembly, July 12, 2007, on Indian and Northern Affairs website http://72.14.209.104/search?/q=cache:itEsF3DuisJ:www.ainc.gc/spch/2007/afn (accessed Sept. 18, 2007).

Chapter 1: The Young Man

1 Peter S. Schmalz, *The Ojibwa of Southern Ontario* (Toronto: University of Toronto Press, 1991) 208.

2 Pegahmagabow's original headstone erected by Veterans Affairs Canada gave his age at death as 64, making the year of his birth 1888. His Canadian Expeditionary Force attestation form states his birthdate as March 9, 1891, but Marie Anderson said March 9, 1889, is correct.

3 LAC, RG 10, vol. 2572, file 116331-pt. 0 (Reel C-12787), "Parry Sound Indian Superintendent is Reporting the Death of Michael Pegamagabo [sic] and he is asking for authority to enter the names of his Widow and Son on the Parry Island Band Paylist, 1891," Dr. Thomas S. Walton to Deputy Superintendent of Indian Affairs L. Vankoughnet, May 26, 1891.

4 Ibid., Walton to Vankoughnet, Oct. 24, 1891.

5 LAC, RG 10, vol. 2761, file 151286 (Reel C-12792), "Parry Sound Superintendency, Minutes of council meetings, requisitions and accounts of the Parry Island and Nipissing Bands," Dr. Thomas Smith Walton to Deputy Superintendent of Indian Affairs Hayter Reed, July 10, 1894, and William Brown Maclean to Indian Affairs, March 24, 1899.

6 Taped personal interview with Duncan Pegahmagabow, Jan. 5, 1990.

7 Taped personal interview with Marie Anderson, Feb. 2, 2005.

8 John Steckley and Bryan Cummins, "Pegahmagabow of Parry Island: From Jenness Informant to Individual," *The Canadian Journal of Native Studies* XXV.1 (2005): 36.

9 Diamond Jenness, *The Ojibwa Indians of Parry Island: Their Social and Religious Life* (Ottawa: King's Printer, 1935) 97.

10 Ibid. 76.

11 Ibid. 83.

12 Marie Anderson, Feb. 2, 2005.

13 Jenness 81. There were three different types of medicine men, of which the *kusabindugeyu* was considered the least powerful. He had the gift of being able to recognize the source of a disease. He did not use herbal medicines, other than as a layman or member of the Midewiwin.

14 Ibid. 68. *Medewadji* are *manido* (spirits) of the *djiskan* (shaking tent) who assist the *djiskiu*, considered to be the most powerful of the medicine men. Author Jordan D. Paper writes that shaking tent rituals continue on Anishnabe and Cree reserves and those who can perform them are highly respected. See *Native North American Religious Traditions: Dancing for Life* (Greenwood Publishing Group, 2007) 142.

15 Steckley and Cummins 40.

16 Jenness 48.

17 John H. Blackmore, MP, to Pegahmagabow, May 12, 1951. The author is greatly indebted to the late Duncan Pegahmagabow for giving him access to his father's letters and personal papers. Further references to this collection are noted as Pegahmagabow papers (PP).

18 PP, Undated biographical sketch in Francis Pegahmagabow's own handwriting.

19 Jenness 94.

20 Ibid.

21 Duncan Pegahmagabow, Jan. 5, 1990.

22 LAC, RG 10, vol. 9505 (Reel C-7168), "Parry Island Robinson Treaty Payments, 1871–1893."

23 AO, MS 137 (Vol. 1), Parry Island Reserve Records. This microfilm includes an account of Pegahmagabow's life, in his own handwriting. Access to these records is restricted by the Wasauksing First Nation band council. The author consulted copies of the original records at the home of Franz Koennecke on Jan. 30, 1999. Mr. Koennecke, who passed away suddenly on Nov. 16, 1999, was employed by the Georgian Bay/French River Treaty Unit.

24 PP, Walter Lockwood Haight to Chief Peter Megis, Dec. 19, 1911.

25 AO, MS 396 (Reel 7), Duncan Fraser Macdonald diaries, entry for Jan. 16, 1912.

26 Duncan Pegahmagabow, Jan. 5, 1990.

27 PP, Sister Benedict of St. Joseph's Hospital to Pegahmagabow, June 18, 1914.

28 PP, Father Gaston Artus, S.J., to Pegahmagabow, June 16, 1914.

Chapter 2: The Warrior

1 Edward Benton-Banai, *The Mishomis Book: The Voice of the Ojibwa* (Red School House, 1988) 76.

2 Jenness 8. Pegahmagabow told Jenness: "My clan is the caribou. I have never visited Temogami [sic], but I have heard there are caribou people there also, and if I ever wish to spend a winter in that district I shall seek them out and ask them to use their influence with their band so that it will assign me a good hunting ground. They are my relatives and will certainly help me." The dodem (clans) represented on Parry Island in 1929 were the caribou, beaver, otter, loon, hawk and eagle. Membership in a dodem is inherited patrilineally with prescriptive exogamy. The Ojibwa, Potawatomi, and Odawa share dodem and members of the same clan thought of themselves as close relatives even if their tribal group differed.

3 "Prince and Pegahmagabow," *Toronto Evening Telegram* Aug. 28, 1919: 13.

4 James W. St. G. Walker, "Race and Recruitment in World War I: Enlist-

ment of Visible Minorities in the Canadian Expeditionary Force," *Canadian Historical Review* LXX.1 (March 1989): 2–24.

5   L. James Dempsey, *Warriors of the King: Prairie Indians in World War I* (University of Regina, 1999), "Appendix A: Prairie Indian Enlistees of World War I" 85–102.

6   James Dempsey, "The Indians and World War One," *Alberta History* XXXI.3 (Summer 1983): 1–8; Gaffen 20.

7   LAC, RG 10, vol. 6766, file 452-13 (Reel C-8511), "War 1914–1918, Reports and Correspondence regarding recruits and enlisted Indians, 1914–1918," Surgeon General to Deputy Minister of Indian Affairs Duncan Campbell Scott, Oct. 22, 1915.

8   LAC, RG 150, Acc. 199-93/166, Box 7701-23, Personnel record of #6848 Cpl. Francis Pegahmagabow.

9   "Brig.-Gen. Frederic William Hill," *Who Was Who, 1951–1960* (London: Adam and Charles Black, 1964) 520.

10 *Parry Sound North Star* Sept. 3, 1914: 5.

11 John Macfie, "A fighting man called 'Peggy' was a war hero," *Georgian Bay Beacon* Nov. 11, 1982: A3. Reprinted in *Now and Then: Footnotes to Parry Sound History* (Parry Sound: Beacon Publishing Company, 1983) 107–9.

12 Duncan Fraser Macdonald to John Bellamy Miller, Nov. 17, 1914. Letter provided to the author by John Macfie.

13 PP, Elizabeth Smith of Claremont, Ont., to Alexander Logan, Apr. 3, 1920.

14 LAC, RG 9 III (Reel T-10704), War diary of the 1st Battalion, CEF, February 1915.

15 1st Battalion war diary, Appendix 1 of Apr. 1915, Narrative of operations Apr. 23–30, 1915; G.W.L. Nicholson, *Canadian Expeditionary Force, 1914–1919,* (Ottawa: Queen's Printer, 1964) 67–71.

16 Edgar Wackett, "Experiences with the Western Ontario Regiment, Canadian Expeditionary Force," Waterloo Historical Society, *Fifth Annual Report,* (Kitchener: Waterloo Historical Society, 1917) 46.

17 Daniel G. Dancocks, *Welcome to Flanders, the First Canadian Battle of the Great War: Ypres, 1915* (Toronto: McClelland and Stewart, 1988) 144–5.

18 Jenness 53. A recent book that refers to Pegahmagabow as the "Indian Sgt. York" has a different version of this quote: "I have no idea what was in it. Sometimes it felt hard as a rock, other times it seemed to be empty. At night it seemed to be rising and falling like it could breathe. I kept it with me at all times and I don't think I could have survived the war without it." See Al Carroll, *Medicine Bags & Dog Tags: American Indian Veterans from Colonial Times to the Second Iraq War* (University of Nebraska Press, 2008) 111. Daughter Marie Anderson said the bag was given to her father by Jean King.

19 Taped personal interview with Levi Nanibush, Jan. 25, 1991.

20 Macfie, *Georgian Bay Beacon.*

21 Leslie P. Mepham, "Making Their Mark: Canadian Snipers and the Great War, 1914–1918," M.A. thesis (University of Windsor, 1997) 37.

22 Copies of the *North Star* for 1962 are not available on microfilm. Clipping provided to the author by John Macfie.

23 Mepham 75–9.

24 Cpl. Richard Miller of the 1st Battalion, CEF, became the first Canadian to be awarded the MM for gallantry under heavy bombardment near Wulvershem on March 18, 1916. He had been recommended for the Distinguished Conduct Medal. Promoted sergeant, he was subsequently killed in action on July 9, 1916, at the age of 27. He is buried at Woods Cemetery, Zillebeke, Belgium. LAC, RG 9 III, vol. 4690, folder 46, file 5, "Individual Narrative. Account of exploit of #400749 Cpl. R. Miller near Wulvershem," as well a letter from Harry Abbink to the author, July 17, 1989.

25 Harry and Cindy Abbink, *The Military Medal Canadian Recipients, 1916–1922* (Calgary: Alison Publishing Company, 1987) vii.

26 Pierre Berton, *Vimy* (Toronto: McClelland and Stewart, 1986) 281.

27 LAC, RG 10, vol. 6771, file 452-30 (Reel C-8515), "War 1914-1918, Correspondence regarding lists of returned Indian soldiers, 1919–1920," Alexander Logan to Indian Affairs, May 20, 1919.

28 "Prince and Pegahmagabow," *Toronto Evening Telegram*.

29 The elusive Military Medal citation was provided to the author by John Beaucage, who at the time was chief of Wasauksing First Nation. Beaucage had purchased a number of official CEF documents auctioned through the eBay website in March 2003. At the time, he said the seller was evasive a   how he came to have possession of the documents. The Museum could not provide a logical explanation for the documents being in private hands rather than in an archival repository such as Library and Archives Canada.

30 Pegahmagabow's personnel record.

31 1st Battalion war diary, September 1916.

32 LAC, RG 10, vol. 3181, file 124-1A (Reel C-11335), Pegahmagabow to Indian Affairs, March 8, 1917. Pegahmagabow did not drink alcohol and abhorred drunkenness. Parry Sound Indian agent D.F. Macdonald recorded in his personal diary on Sept. 30, 1911: "Frank Pegamahgabo [sic] reported John King and Mike Moses drunk on Parry Island. I sent Frank up to police magistrate [Joseph] Farrer to get a warrant out for them."

33 *Parry Sound North Star* Dec. 7, 1916: 5.

34 LAC, RG 150, Acc. 1992-93/166, Box 8222-38, Personnel record of #657321 Pte. Isaac Rice, 162nd Battalion, CEF.

35 Nikolas Gardner, "The Great War and Waterloo County: The travails of the 118th Overseas Battalion," *Ontario History* LXXXIX.3 (September 1987): 220.

36 LAC, RG 10, vol. 1735, file 63-22, p.2 (Reel C-15022), "Minutes of council—

Oka, Pointe Bleue, Parry Sound," Parry Island band council resolution of Apr. 2, 1917.

37 Daniel G. Dancocks, *Legacy of Valour: The Canadians at Passchendaele* (Edmonton: Hurtig Publishers, 1986) 165.

38 Pegahmagabow's personnel record.

39 LAC, RG 10, vol. 6792, file 452-557 (Reel C-8526), "Parry Sound Agency, Parry Island Band, War Record of Corporal Francis Pegamagabou (Chief Ojibwa Tribe), Military Medal and two bars, pension, 1919–1941," Pegahmagabow to Department of National Defence, Oct. 19, 1934.

40 John Macfie to the author, Nov. 3, 1989.

41 PP, Cecilia Oldmeadow to Pegahmagabow, Apr. 2, 1918.

42 1st Battalion war diary, Appendix to August 1914, includes four-page summary of operations, Lt.-Col. A.W. Sparling to GOC 1st Canadian Infantry Brigade, Aug. 13, 1918.

43 Ibid., entry for Aug. 30, 1918.

44 Wasauksing First Nation Chief John Beaucage provided the author with the citation for the second bar. See endnote 29.

45 VAC, Pension file #126927, Cpl. Francis Pegahmagabow.

46 Pegahmagabow's personnel record.

47 In January 1916, Lt.-Col. Hill had been promoted brigadier-general and given command of the 9th Brigade of the newly formed 3rd Canadian Division. Hill's replacement, Lt.-Col. Frank Albert Creighton, was killed when a shell hit the dugout where he was meeting with other officers during the fighting at Mount Sorrel in June 1916. Lt.-Col. Albert Walter Sparling, a former major in the 10th Battalion, commanded from August 1917 to 1919, taking over from Lt.-Col. George Cuthbert Hodson.

48 Daniel G. Dancocks, *Gallant Canadians: The Story of the Tenth Canadian Infantry Battalion, 1914–1919* (Calgary: The Calgary Highlanders Regimental Funds Association, 1990) 114.

49 PP, rough draft of a letter Pegahmagabow sent to Brig.-Gen. Frederic W. Hill, Feb. 20, 1932.

50 Pegahmagabow's personnel record.

Chapter 3: The Returned Hero

1 *Parry Sound North Star* May 15, 1919: 5.

2 *Parry Sound North Star* June 19, 1919: 5; AO, MS 932 (Reel 501), Marriage registration #20871 of 1919.

3 LAC, RG 10, vol. 1735, file 63-22, pt.2, Logan to Indian Affairs, Sept. 14, 1914, enclosing Parry Island band council resolution of Sept. 14, 1914.

4 LAC, RG 10, vol. 6767, file 452-15, pt.1 (Reel C-8512), "War 1914–1918, Applications made by Indians for Discharges from the Armed Forces, 1915–1920," Chief Peter Megis and council to the Governor General, Dec. 28, 1916; LAC, RG 150, Acc. 1992-93/166, Box 5887-12, Personnel record of #657377 Pte. Simpson John Manitowaba, 162nd Battalion, CEF.

5 LAC, RG 10, vol. 452-15, pt.1, Chief Peter Megis to Duncan Campbell Scott, Aug. 7, 1918. A military personnel record for Henry Medwayosh could not be located at LAC. Access to information and privacy analyst Tony Bonacci to the author, Nov. 10, 1997.

6 LAC, RG 10, vol. 6792, file 452-557, Alexander Logan to Indian Affairs, Aug. 15, 1919.

7 "Prince and Pegahmagabow," *Toronto Evening Telegram*.

8 "Pegahmagabow is Decorated by Prince Edward," *Parry Sound North Star* Sept. 4, 1919: 1.

9 *Annual Report of The Department of Indian Affairs For The Year Ended March 31, 1919* (Ottawa: King's Printer, 1920) 15.

10 Taped personal interview with Lyle Jones, Jan. 24, 1991.

11 VAC, Pegahmagabow's pension file, Stanley B. Coristine, Board of Pension Commissioners, to Dr. Wood. Nov. 28, 1919.

12 LAC, RG 10, vol. 7502, file 25022-5 (Reel C-14790), "Parry Sound Agency, Soldier Settlement, Francis Pegahmagabow, 1919–1935," Alexander Logan to Indian Affairs, Jan. 8, 1920.

13 Franz M. Koennecke, "Wasoksing: The History of Parry Island, an Anishnabwe Community in the Georgian Bay, 1850 to 1920," M.A. thesis (University of Waterloo, 1984) 26.

14 LAC, RG 10, vol. 7502, file 25022-5, Pegahmagabow to Soldiers' Aid Commission, Oct.15, 1919.

15 Ibid., Alexander Logan to Indian Affairs, Jan. 5, 1920.

16 Ibid.

17 Ibid., Elijah Tabobondung to Deputy Superintendent-General Duncan Campbell Scott, March 6, 1920.

18 LAC, RG 10, Series B-3, vol. 7376, file 16022-17, Alexander Logan to Indian Affairs, Nov. 4, 1920.

19 "Pegahmagabow now Parry Island chief," *Parry Sound North Star*, Feb. 3, 1921: 1.

20 LAC, RG 10, vol. 7663, file 22022-5 (Reel C-11608), "Parry Sound Agency, Right of way for Ottawa, Arnprior, and Parry Sound Railway Company through a portion of the Parry Island Reserve." See also Koennecke 243–9.

21 LAC, RG 10, Series B-3, vol. 7376, file 16022-17, Alexander Logan to Indian Affairs, Apr. 8, 1921.

22 PP, undated biographical sketch in Francis Pegahmagabow's own handwriting. In addition, see Robin Jarvis Brownlie, *A Fatherly Eye: Indian Agents, Government Power and Aboriginal Resistance in Ontario, 1918–1939* (Toronto: Oxford

University Press, 2003) 65. Brownlie also refers to Pegahmagabow's belief that he had been chosen to free his people from "white slavery."

23 LAC, RG 10, vol. 7540, file 29022-5 (Reel C-14810), "Parry Sound Agency, Surrender of certain land on the Parry Island Reserve in 1900." See also Koennecke 249–52.

24 "Car Ferries Being Built for Depot Passengers," *Parry Sound North Star* Apr. 13, 1933: 1.

25 PP, Pegahmagabow to Indian Affairs, June 2, 1925.

26 "Parry Island Has Garnet and Mica Mine," *Parry Sound North Star* Feb. 3, 1921: 1.

27 LAC, RG 10, vol. 7460, file 18022-5, pt.1 (Reel C-14763), "Parry Sound Agency, Prospecting for minerals on Parry Island Reserve, 1899–1946," H.J. Bury to Superintendent General Duncan Campbell Scott, May 8, 1929.

28 PP, Parry Island council resolution, June 9, 1923.

29 PP, Boving Hydraulic & Engineering Company Ltd. to Pegahmagabow, May 7, 1925. In the summer of 1919, the Town of Parry Sound accepted a $19,270 tender from the company to provide hydraulic equipment for a new hydro-electric generating plant on the Seguin River. See Adrian Hayes, "The Day the Dam Burst," in *Parry Sound: Gateway to Northern Ontario* (Toronto: Natural Heritage Books, 2005) 135–45.

30 LAC, RG 10, Vol. 10279, File 475/8-8-8-16 (Reel T-7565), "Parry Sound Agency, Correspondence regarding the electric power services on Parry Island Reserve No. 16, 1925–1966," Acting assistant deputy secretary A.F. Mackenzie to John M. Daly, March 11, 1925.

31 Norman D. Shields, "Anishinabek Political Alliance in the Post-Confederation Period: The Grand General Indian Council of Ontario, 1870–1936," M.A. thesis (Kingston: Queen's University, 2001) ii.

32 Shields 128; LAC, RG 10, vol. 2641, file 129690-3A, Alexander Logan to secretary of Indian Affairs J.D. McLean, May 20, 1919, enclosing minutes of Parry Island council meeting, May 3, 1919.

33 Kulchyski, "A Considerable Unrest"; Jean Goodwill and Norma Sluman, *John Tootoosis: A Biography of a Cree Leader* (Winnipeg: Pemmican Publications, 1984) 128–36.

34 LAC, RG 10, vol. 3211, file 527787, pt.1 (Reel C-11340), "Formation of a Canadian League of Indians by F.O. Loft of the Six Nations Band, 1919–1935," Duncan Campbell Scott to Senator Sir James Lougheed, Feb. 21, 1921.

35 Ibid., Alexander Logan to Indian Affairs, Sept. 18, 1919, and secretary of Indian Affairs J.D. McLean to Alexander Logan, Sept. 23, 1919.

36 *Parry Sound North Star* June 9, 1921: 4.

37 AO, MS-137, Parry Island council resolution passed Feb. 2, 1922.

38 Ibid., Pegahmagabow to Frederick O. Loft, Jan. 1, 1922.

39 LAC, RG 10, vol. 9182, Department of Indian Affairs establishment book,

outside service, A-G, 1880–1955, Appointment of John McLean Daly on Sept. 22, 1922.

40 Taped personal interview with James Edward Wheatley, Jan. 25, 1991.

41 LAC, RG 150, Acc. 1992-93/166, Box 2276-55, Personnel record of #648222 Sgt. John McLean Daly, 7th Battalion Canadian Overseas Railway Construction Corps, CEF.

42 With his first wife, Daly had in all eight surviving children.

43 *Parry Sound North Star*, Daly's obituary, Nov. 11, 1943: 2.

44 Robin Brownlie, "Man on the Spot: John Daly, Indian Agent in Parry Sound, 1922-1939," *Journal of the Canadian Historical Association* 5 (1994): 74.

45 Robin Jarvis Brownlie, *A Fatherly Eye* 57.

46 LAC, RG 10, vol. 7927, file 32-22 (Reel C-13504), "Parry Sound Agency, Elections of Chiefs and Councillors, 1903–1925," Indian agent John M. Daly to secretary of Indian Affairs J.D. McLean, Apr. 3, 1925.

47 Paul Williams, "The Chain," LLM thesis (Toronto: York University, 1982) 21.

48 LAC, RG 10, Vol. 8021, File 475/37-7-5-9, "Affairs of Chief Francis Pegahmagabow, No. 9 Parry Island Band, Parry Sound Agency," secretary of Indian Affairs J.D. McLean to John M. Daly, June 10, 1924.

49 LAC, RG 10, vol. 7927, file 32-22, John M. Daly to J.D. McLean, Feb. 9, 1924.

50 PRO, HO 374/33030, personnel record of #314257 Capt. John Roland Hett, 1st North Midland Brigade, Royal Field Artillery.

51 "Mail Robbers Kill Farmer, Wound Two Men," *Toronto Daily Star* Aug. 18, 1928: 1.

52 PP, John Roland Hett to Pegahmagabow, Feb. 2, 1925.

53 LAC, RG 10, Vol. 3161, File 363644 (Reel C-11332), "Parry Sound Superintendency, Claim of Parry Island Band to Four Square Miles Opposite of the Parry Island Reserve Within the Town of Parry Sound, 1910–1936," Pegahmagabow to John M. Daly, March 9, 1936.

54 LAC, RG 10, Vol. 7927, File 32-22, H.J. Bury to Secretary of Indian Affairs J.D. McLean, Mar. 20, 1922.

55 Taped personal interview with Stewart King, Feb. 2, 2005.

56 LAC, RG 10, vol. 7927, file 32-22, Secretary of Indian Affairs J.D. McLean to Alexander Logan, Dec. 28, 1921, enclosing petition dated Dec. 7, 1921.

57 Ibid., H.J. Bury to J.D. McLean, Mar. 22, 1922, enclosing petitions dated Mar. 22, 1922 and Dec. 7, 1921.

58 Ibid., John M. Daly to J.D. McLean, Mar. 14, 1925, enclosing petition dated Mar. 10, 1925.

59 Ibid., John M. Daly to J.D. McLean, Apr. 3, 1925.

60 Ibid., Councillor John Miller to Indian Affairs, Apr. 14, 1925.

61 Ibid., John M. Daly to J.D. McLean, Aug. 24, 1925, enclosing Pegahmagabow's

resignation dated Aug. 21, 1925; LAC, RG 10, vol. 7927, file 32-22 (Reel C-13504), "Parry Sound Agency, Elections of Chiefs and Councillors, 1926–1937," John M. Daly to J.D. McLean, Jan. 12, 1926.

Chapter 4: The Disilllusioned Veteran

1 "F. Pegamagobow [sic] on guard duty at Ottawa and Toronto," *Parry Sound North Star* May 25, 1939: 1.
2 PP, Undated biographical sketch in Francis Pegahmagabow's own handwriting. He refers to having "the honor to escort" King George VI and Queen Elizabeth at Ottawa, Toronto, and Sudbury.
3 PP, Brig.-Gen. Frederic W. Hill to Pegahmagabow, Oct. 10, 1925.
4 LAC, RG 24, vol. 197, Regimental History of the 23rd Northern Pioneers.
5 According to the 1st Battalion, CEF, nominal roll, the other two were Lieut. Kenneth Arnold Mahaffy of Bracebridge and Lieut. Christopher Waterhouse Hodgson.
6 LAC, RG 150, Acc. 1992-93/166, Box 5328-49, Personnel record of Lt.-Col. William James Austin Lalor.
7 Taped telephone interview with Roy Lloyd O'Halloran, Jan. 6, 2003.
8 Macfie, *Sons of the Pioneers* 74–5.
9 *Parry Sound North Star*, "Military Notes," Sept. 3, 1936: 1.
10 Duncan Pegahmagbow, Jan. 5,1990.
11 VAC, Pegahmagabow's pension file, Dr. Kenneth Andrew Denholm to Medical Representative, The Canadian Legion of the British Empire Service League, Mar. 26, 1930.
12 Ibid., Pegahmagabow to the Canadian Pension Commission, June 1, 1940.
13 Marie Anderson, Feb. 2, 2005.
14 Marie Anderson, Feb. 2, 2005, and taped personal interview with Priscilla Pegahmagabow, Feb. 2, 2005.
15 Marie Anderson, Feb. 2, 2005. Although the death of Leo James Pegahmagabow was documented by the Department of Pensions and National Health, it was not registered with the Ontario Registrar-General and no death certificate was issued. Records kept by the funeral home Logan's of Parry Sound confirm the child was buried on July 1, 1925, by former Indian agent Alexander Logan. The Ontario director of vital statistics wrote to Logan on May 7, 1930, inquiring who issued the burial permit.
16 Taped personal interview with Levi Nanibush, Jan. 25, 1991.
17 Duncan Pegahmagabow, Jan. 5, 1990.
18 Marie Anderson, Feb. 2, 2005.
19 Ibid. Robert Henry Pegahmagabow was last seen in the area of the Kipling

Hotel in Parry Sound on Aug. 15, 1962. His boat was found the next morning in the harbour and the Ontario Provincial Police believed he may have drowned in an attempt to return to Parry Island. No body was recovered and he's still listed as a missing person.

20 Jenness v.

21 LAC, RG 10, Series B-3, Vol. 7376, File 16022-17, Samuel Devlin to Indian Affairs, Jan. 19, 1945.

22 Jenness 86–7.

23 Ibid. 87. John Manitowaba was about 70 when interviewed by Jenness in 1929. John M. Daly wrote that there was almost universal dissatisfaction on Parry Island after residents elected Manitowaba chief in February 1933. Daly tried unsuccessfully to convince his superiors to remove Manitowaba from office for incompetence. In a move supportive of Daly, Pegahmagabow, as a member of council, introduced motion to have Manitowaba deposed as chief.

24 VAC, Pegahmagabow's pension file, Recommendation for award of pension, Apr. 9, 1930.

25 A fifth son, Paul Anthony Pegahmagabow, died from cholera on July 18, 1927, when he was less than a month old. AO, MS 935 (Reel 351), Death registration #26,400 of 1927.

26 VAC, Pegahmagabow's pension file, Pegahmagabow to Department of Pensions and National Health, Jan. 18, 1932.

27 *Parry Sound North Star* Sept. 24, 1931: 4.

28 Brownlie, *A Fatherly Eye* 69.

29 Ibid. 81–4.

30 Ibid. 82. John M. Daly to Joseph Partridge, March 1, 1935.

31 LAC, RG 10, Vol. 6772, File 452-40 (Reel C-8515), "War 1914–1918, Correspondence regarding relief allowances to veteran Indians receiving insufficient pensions, 1936–1943," John M. Daly to Indian Affairs, June 9, 1936.

32 Ibid., John M. Daly to Indian Affairs, Jan. 11, 1934.

33 Schmalz, *The Ojibwa of Southern Ontario* 233.

34 PP, rough draft of a letter Pegahmagabow wrote to Brig.-Gen. Frederic W. Hill, Feb. 20, 1932. The drain that his sons' education put on his finances is evident in an Oct. 5, 1933, letter to Pegahmagabow from Sister Perpetua (Greenan): "I intend to make a list of what I bought your boys last year with the money you sent. I thought from what William said, you were not satisfied. You know they go to school to the Sisters. The school is close to [St. Peter's] Cathedral and we have to keep them well. I bought each about four pair of shoes a year for two years. That is eight pair each, which means 16 pair and about four pair of rubbers..." See Brownlie, *A Fatherly Eye* 132. According to Brownlie, Pegahmagabow sent his sons to the orphanage for schooling after considerable urging by Indian agent John M. Daly. "Until this time Pegahmagabow had resisted sending his children to school and even managed

to prevent them from attending the reserve school, which was Protestant," Brownlie wrote.

35 Macfie, *Sons of the Pioneers* 74.

36 VAC, Pegahmagabow's pension file, Dr. G.C. Anglin to Dr. A.C. Rowswell at the Department of Pensions and National Health, Feb. 19, 1940. Dr. Anglin noted: "I would judge his bronchitis is rather more than when he was last here, but even so it is not in itself grossly disabling. He should be able to carry out many light types of work. Guard duty under reasonably favorable circumstances should not be beyond his capacity."

37 PP, pocket diary entry for June 7, 1945. On May 4, 1945, Pegahmagabow wrote: "They found matches on me. Laid off seven days. I wanted the week off any way."

38 "Military Medal, Two Bars and 378 Scalps," *Nobel News* Aug. 21, 1943: 6.

39 Gaffen, *Forgotten Soldiers* 67.

40 PP, Lt.-Col. J.P. Richards to Pegahmagabow, Aug. 21, 1941.

41 LAC, RG 10, vol. 8021, file 475/37-7-8-9, Pegahmagabow to Prime Minister William Lyon Mackenzie King, Oct. 8, 1941.

42 LAC genealogy and personnel records consultant Louise Brazeau to the author, May 4, 1998. As William J. Pegahmagabow died in 1991, his military personnel record will not be open for research until 2011.

43 PP, William J. Pegahmagabow to Francis Pegahmagabow, Oct. 3, 1943.

44 PP, William J. Pegahmagabow to Michael A. Pegahmagabow, Apr. 7, 1944.

45 LAC, RG 10, vol. 6767, file 452-15, p.2 (Reel C-8512), "War 1939, Applications made by Indians for discharges from Active Service in the Armed Forces, 1941–1946," Michael A. Pegahmagabow to Indian Affairs, Aug. 12, 1942.

46 Ibid., Samuel Devlin to Indian Affairs, Aug. 18, 1942.

47 LAC, Personnel record of #B-111510 Pte. Michael A. Pegahmagabow; "Chief Dies From Gunshot Wound," *Parry Sound North Star* Aug. 11, 1955: 1. Michael Pegahmagabow died tragically in August 1955 as the result of a bullet wound in the abdomen, while serving as chief of the Parry Island band. According to newspaper reports at the time, he was preparing to get into his boat to go to the Glen Burney Lodge, where he was employed as a guide, and his rifle accidentally discharged.

Chapter 5: The Indian Activist

1 Laura Eggertson, "Ottawa elevates natives to 'nation'," *Toronto Star* Jan. 7, 1998: A7.

2 Laura Eggertson, "'Profound regret' offered for Canada's native policy," *Toronto Star* Jan. 8, 1998: A1.

3 Laurie Meijer Drees, "Introduction to Documents One to Five: Nationalism, the League of Nations and the Six Nations of Grand River," *Native Studies Review* X.1, (1995): 75–7.

4 Barbara Graymont, *Fighting Tuscarora: The Autobiography of Chief Clinton Rickard* (Syracuse University Press, 1973) 132.

5 LAC, RG 10, vol. 3212, file 527787-4 (Reel C-11341), "Headquarters, Indian Conventions Held in Ottawa on Oct. 19–21, 1943 and June 5–7, 1944, General Correspondence," Director of Indian Affairs Dr. Harold W. McGill to the deputy minister, Sept. 25, 1943. For more on Jules Sioui see Hugh Shewell, "Jules Sioui and Indian Political Radicalism in Canada, 1943-1944," *Journal of Canadian Studies* XXXIV.3 (Fall 1999): 211–42.

6 Ibid., circular letter to all Indian agents, inspectors of Indian agencies, and the Indian commissioner for British Columbia, from Dr. Harold W. McGill, director of Indian Affairs, Sept. 24, 1943.

7 LAC, RG 10, series B-3, vol. 7376, file 16022-17, Arthur Graeme Slaght to John M. Daly, May 29, 1939.

8 LAC, RG 150, Acc. 1992-93/166, Box 2489-61, Personnel record of #1260274 Pte. Samuel Devlin, 4th Divisional Ammunition Column, CEF. In Apr. 1920, Devlin married Mildred Armstrong, the daughter of Parry Sound-area lumberman William James Armstrong. They had three daughters. *Parry Sound North Star*, Devlin's obituary, Nov. 9, 1961: 6.

9 VAC, Pegahmagabow's pension file, Pegahmagabow to the Canadian Pension Commission, Jan. 22, 1941.

10 "Indian Delegation Will Attempt to Interview Mr. King," *Ottawa Evening Citizen* Oct. 19, 1943: 12.

11 LAC, RG 10, vol. 3212, file 527,787-4, acting director of Indian Affairs R.A. Hoey to Samuel Devlin, Oct. 27, 1943.

12 "Indian Hero drops in on Parliament Hill," *Vancouver Sun* Oct. 25, 1943: 13; "Indian Chief Buys First Large Poppy," *Ottawa Citizen* Oct. 25, 1943: 2.

13 Robert Scott Sheffield, "Winning the War, Winning the Peace: The Image of the 'Indian' in English Canada, 1930–1948," Ph.D. thesis (Waterloo: Wilfrid Laurier University, 2000) 135.

14 LAC, RG 10, vol. 7700, file 23022-5, pt.1 (Reel C-12011), "Parry Sound Agency—Correspondence, labour returns and accounts concerning road work on the Parry Island Reserve, 1896–1935," Report of RCMP Cpl. H.S. Traves, Jan. 16, 1935, Forwarded to the deputy superintendent-general by Insp. R. Armitage of the RCMP Criminal Investigation Branch.

15 LAC, RG 10, vol. 8021, file 474/37-7-8-9, Pegahmagabow to William Barker, Apr. 4, 1941.

16 Ibid., Pegahmagabow to Prime Minister William Lyon Mackenzie King, Mar. 3, 1944.

17 Ibid., Samuel Devlin to Indian Affairs, Mar. 16, 1944.

18 Ibid., Pegahmagabow to British High Commissioner Malcolm McDonald, Apr. 4, 1944.

19 Ibid., Secretary of Indian Affairs T.R.L. MacInnes to J.J.S. Garner, High Commissioner for the United Kingdom, Apr. 13, 1944.

20 LAC, RG 10, vol. 3312, file 527787-4, Circular letter to all Indian Agents..., from acting director of Indian Affairs R.A. Hoey, May 25, 1944.

21 Goodwill and Sluman, *John Tootoosis* 180.

22 E. Palmer Patterson II, "Andrew Paull (1892–1959): Finding a Voice For a New Indian," *Western Canadian Journal of Anthropology* VI.2 (1976).

23 "Certificate for Indians Proposed," *Ottawa Evening Citizen* June 19, 1945: 10.

24 "Indians on Hill," *Ottawa Evening Citizen* June 21, 1945: 1.

25 LAC, RG 10, vol. 6826, file 496-3-2 (Reel C-8546), "Reports and clippings on North American Indian Brotherhood, North American National Government, National Indian Government, 1944–1948," Report of the North American Indian Brotherhood Convention in Ottawa, Sept. 10, 11, and 12, 1945, as printed in a special supplement to *The Indian Missionary Record* Oct. 1945: 3.

26 Ibid.

27 PP, Minutes of first joint session of the Indian Organization Council, held in the convention room of the Detroit YMCA, Sept. 14, 1945. Also a copy of the petition to Prime Minister Mackenzie King dated Sept. 15, 1945.

28 PP, Pegahmagabow's handwritten comments on the back of Jules Sioui's eight-point "Ultimatum" to Canadian Secretary of State Paul Martin, dated June 27, 1947.

29 LAC, RG 10, vol. 6826, file 496-3-2, Minutes of Union of Ontario Indians meeting at Parry Island, Aug. 19–20, 1946, as recorded by Samuel Devlin.

30 "Powwow at YMCA, Indians Hit the Warpath Against Regimentation," *Detroit Free Press*, Sept. 11, 1946: 1, and *Toronto Star* Sept. 12, 1946: 23.

31 Richard R.H. Lueger, "A History of Indian Associations in Canada, 1870–1970," M.A. thesis (Ottawa: Carleton University, Institute of Canadian Studies, 1977) 159–60.

32 PP, Chief John Twain to Pegahmagabow, Oct. 20, 1944.

33 "Alleged Beating Leads to Indian Woman's Death," *Manitoulin Expositor* June 20, 1946: 1 and *Manitoulin Expositor* July 4, 1946: 9

34 PP, Ed Kitchikeg to Pegahmagabow, Aug. 2, 1946, and Oct. 11, 1946.

35 "Provincial Government Says Indians Must Obey Game Laws," *Sudbury Daily Star* Feb. 15, 1940: 9 and "Indians Lose Treaty Rights," *Parry Sound North Star* Apr. 3, 1940: 1.

36 "Ontario Still Ontario—Even for Indian Trapper," *Sudbury Daily Star* May 14, 1946: 1 and "Indians to Appeal," May 21, 1946: 1.

37 "Indians Launch Protest at Secret Council Session," *Sudbury Daily Star* Oct. 15, 1946: 9.

38 Lueger 161.

39 "Hurons Bounce Starving 'Chief'," *Indian Missionary Record* Vol. 13, No. 5, (May, 1950): 1.

40 "Sudbury to Host Gathering of Indian Chiefs," *Sudbury Daily Star* Sept. 22, 1950: 1 and "Indians Turn to UN for Recognition," Sept. 23, 1950: 1.

41 "Would Take Problems to King," *Sudbury Daily Star* Sept. 23, 1950: 3.

42 Marie Anderson, Feb. 2, 2005.

43 "Indian war veteran dies," *Parry Sound North Star* Aug. 7, 1952: 1. In an interview on Jan. 5, 1990, Duncan Pegahmagabow said his father died of a heart attack. However, former Canadian War Museum historian Fred Gaffen and former *Georgian Bay Beacon* columnist John Macfie wrote that he died from a respiratory ailment related to his war service.

44 "Father a great warrior, and so much more," *Parry Sound North Star* May 3, 2000: 4.

45 "Honouring the Algonquin Regiment and one of its finest," *Parry Sound North Star* July 30, 2003: 1.

46 Taped telephone interview with Merle Pegahmagabow, Feb. 24, 2005.

47 "More available about Native soldiers," *Parry Sound North Star* May 10, 2000: 4.

Afterword

1 The first such presentation of Military Medal ribbons by the commanding officer to 14 soldiers is recorded in the 1st Battalion war diary on July 23, 1916. The awards were confirmed in the Aug. 23, 1916, *London Gazette*.

2 LAC, RG 10, vol. 6792, file 452-557.

3 *Annual Report of the Department of Indian Affairs for the Year Ended March 31, 1919* 15.

4 John Macfie, *Georgian Bay Beacon*.

5 Peter Worthington, "No real heroes need apply: Courage in wartime is given short shrift by official Canada," *Toronto Sun* Sept. 21, 2003: 8.

6 Joseph Hall, "Fighting for a warrior's legacy," *Toronto Star* June 4, 2006: D9.

7 Canadian Museum of Civilization website: http://www.civilization.ca/cmc/exhibitions/tresors/treasure/280eng.shtml (accessed Feb. 12, 2009).

8 Summerby, *Native Soldiers, Foreign Battlefields* 11.

9 Veterans Affairs Canada website http://www.vac-acc.gc.ca/remembers/sub.cfm?source=history/other/native/peaceful (accessed Feb. 12, 2009). In a Mar. 22, 1999, letter to the author, senior communications officer Janice Summerby acknowledged that she had made the identification and insisted, "While I cannot state categorically it is him, his records do not rule out the possibil-

ity." On Feb. 25, 2009, Jim Burant, art and photography archives manager at LAC, acknowledged in a letter to the author that there are indeed doubts that Pegahmagabow is in the photo given that he was in England for medical treatment from Nov. 5, 1918, onwards, and was operated on for a hernia at a military hospital in Kirkdale, Liverpool, in February 1919.

10 The Association for Commonwealth Literature and Language Studies website http://ocs.sfu.ca/aclals/viewabstract.php?id=393 (accessed Dec. 30, 2008).

11 *The Globe and Mail*, Letter to the editor, July 10, 2008: A15. Written in response to errors in J.D.M. Stewart, "Honouring our aboriginal sons and daughters," *The Globe and Mail* July 1, 2008: A13.

12 Brig.-Gen. Frederic W. Hill to Pegahmagabow, Nov. 17, 1934.

13 PP, Rough draft of a letter Pegahmagabow sent to Brig.-Gen. Frederic W. Hill, Feb. 20, 1932.

14 Duncan Pegahmagabow, Jan. 5, 1990.

15 James Edward Wheatley and Levi Nanibush, Jan. 25, 1991.

16 PP, Pocket diary entry for Apr. 23, 1950.

17 Petition to Wasauksing First Nation council signed by Duncan Pegahmagabow and Marie Anderson Pegahmagabow dated 2002. Provided to the author by Stewart King on Feb. 2, 2005.

18 Marie Anderson, Feb. 2, 2005.

19 Ibid.

20 Taped telephone interview with Anishinabek Nation Grand Council Chief John Beaucage, Jan. 7, 2009.

21 Stewart King, Feb. 2, 2005.

Sources

Books, articles, and theses

Abbink, Harry, and Cindy Abbink. *The Military Medal Canadian Recipients, 1916–1922.* Calgary: Alison Publishing, 1987.

Benton-Banai, Edward. *The Mishomis Book: The Voice of the Ojibwa.* St. Paul (Minnesota): Red School House/Indian Country Communications, 1988.

Berton, Pierre. *Vimy.* Toronto: McClelland and Stewart, 1986.

Brownlie, Robin. "Man on the Spot: John Daly, Indian Agent in Parry Sound, 1922–1939." *Journal of the Canadian Historical Association* 5 (1994).

———. "Work Hard and Be Grateful: Native Soldier Settlers in Ontario after the First World War." In Franca Iacovetta and Wendy Mitchinson, eds. *On the Case: Explorations in Social History.* Toronto: University of Toronto Press, 1998.

Brownlie, Robin Jarvis. *A Fatherly Eye: Indian Agents, Government Power, and Aboriginal Resistance in Ontario, 1918–1939.* Toronto: Oxford University Press, 2003.

Carroll, Al. *Medicine Bags & Dog Tags: American Indian Veterans from Colonial Times to the Second Iraq War.* Lincoln (Nebraska): University of Nebraska Press, 2008.

Dancocks, Daniel G. *Gallant Canadians: The Story of the Tenth*

Canadian Infantry Battalion, 1914–1919. Calgary: Calgary High-landers Regimental Funds Association, 1990.

————. *Legacy of Valour: The Canadians at Passchendaele.* Edmonton: Hurtig Publishers, 1986.

————. *Welcome to Flanders, The First Canadian Battle of the Great War: Ypres, 1915.* Toronto: McClelland and Stewart, 1988.

Dempsey, James. "The Indians and World War One." *Alberta History* XXXI.3 (Summer 1983): 1–8.

Dempsey, L. James. *Warriors of the King: Prairie Indians in World War I.* Regina: University of Regina, 1999.

Department of Indian Affairs. *Annual Report of The Department of Indian Affairs For The Year Ended March 31, 1919.* Ottawa: King's Printer, 1920.

Drees, Laurie Meijer. "Introduction to Documents One to Five: Nationalism, the League of Nations and the Six Nations of Grand River." *Native Studies Review* X.1 (1995): 75–7.

Gaffen, Fred. *Forgotten Soldiers.* Penticton, B.C.: Theytus Books, 1985.

Gardner, Nikolas. "The Great War and Waterloo County: The Travails of the 118th Overseas Battalion." *Ontario History* LXXXIX.3 (September 1987).

Goodwill, Jean, and Norma Sluman. *John Tootoosis: A Biography of a Cree Leader.* Winnipeg: Pemmican Publications, 1984.

Graymont, Barbara. *Fighting Tuscarora: The Autobiography of Chief Clinton Rickard.* Syracuse: Syracuse University Press, 1973.

Hayes, Adrian. *Parry Sound: Gateway to Northern Ontario.* Toronto: Natural Heritage Books, 2005.

Jenness, Diamond. *The Ojibwa Indians of Parry Island: Their Social and Religious Life.* Ottawa: King's Printer, 1935.

Koennecke, Franz M. "Wasoksing: The History of Parry Island, an Anishnabwe Community in the Georgian Bay, 1850 to 1920." MA thesis, University of Waterloo, 1984.

Kulchyski, Peter. "A Considerable Unrest: F.O. Loft and the

League of Indians." *Native Studies Review* 4.1-2 (1988).

Lueger, Richard R.H. "A History of Indian Associations in Canada, 1870–1970." MA thesis, Carleton University (Ottawa), Institute of Canadian Studies, 1977.

Macfie, John. "A fighting man called 'Peggy' was a war hero." *Georgian Bay Beacon* Nov. 11, 1982: A3. Reprinted in *Now and Then: Footnotes to Parry Sound History*. Parry Sound: Beacon Publishing Company, 1983.

———. *Sons of the Pioneers.* Parry Sound: Hay Press, 2001.

Mepham, Leslie P. "Making Their Mark: Canadian Snipers and the Great War, 1914–1918." MA thesis, University of Windsor, 1997.

Nicholson, G.W.L. *Canadian Expeditionary Force, 1914–1919.* Ottawa: Queen's Printer, 1964.

Paper, Jordan D. *Native North American Religious Traditions: Dancing for Life.* Westport (Connecticut): Greenwood Publishing Group, 2007.

Patterson, E. Palmer, II. "Andrew Paull (1892–1959): Finding a Voice For a New Indian." *Western Canadian Journal of Anthropology* VI.2 (1976).

St. G. Walker, James W. "Race and Recruitment in World War I: Enlistment of Visible Minorities in the Canadian Expeditionary Force." *Canadian Historical Review* LXX.1 (Mar. 1989): 1–24.

Schmalz, Peter S. *The Ojibwa of Southern Ontario.* Toronto: University of Toronto Press, 1991.

Sheffield, Robert Scott. "Winning the War, Winning the Peace: The Image of the 'Indian' in English Canada, 1930–1948." Ph.D. thesis, Wilfrid Laurier University (Waterloo, Ontario), 2000.

Shewell, Hugh. "Jules Sioui and Indian Political Radicalism in Canada, 1943–1944." *Journal of Canadian Studies* XXXIV.3 (Fall 1999): 211–42.

Steckley, John, and Bryan Cummins. "Pegahmagabow of Parry Island: From Jenness Informant to Individual." *The Canadian Journal of Native Studies* XXV.1 (2005).

Sources

Summerby, Janice. *Native Soldiers, Foreign Battlefields*. Ottawa: Veterans Affairs Canada, 1993.

Wackett, Edgar. "Experiences with the Western Ontario Regiment, Canadian Expeditionary Force." *Waterloo Historical Society, Fifth Annual Report*. Kitchener: Waterloo Historical Society, 1917.

Williams, Paul. "The Chain." LLM thesis, York University (Toronto), 1982.

Documents and papers

Archives of Ontario:
    MS 137: Parry Island Reserve Records
    MS 396: Duncan Fraser Macdonald diaries
    MS 935: death registrations
Library and Archives Canada:
    RG 10: Indian Affairs
    RG 9: Militia and Defence
    RG 150: Ministry of the Overseas Military Forces of Canada
Pegahamagabow papers (privately held)
Public Record Office (England): HO 374/33030, personnel record of Capt. John Roland Hett
Veterans Affairs Canada: Francis Pegahmagabow's pension file

Websites

Association for Commonwealth Literature and Language Studies
Canadian Museum of Civilization
Indian and Northern Affairs Canada
Veterans Affairs Canada

Newspapers and miscellaneous periodicals

Detroit Free Press

Georgian Bay Beacon

Globe and Mail (Toronto)

Indian Missionary Record

Kitchener Record

Legion Magazine

Manitoulin Expositor

Nobel News (DIL company pub.)

Ottawa Citizen/Evening Citizen

Parry Sound North Star

Toronto Evening Telegram

Toronto Star/Daily Star

Toronto Sun

Vancouver Sun

Personal communications

Marie Anderson

John Beaucage

Lyle Jones

Stewart King

John Macfie

Levi Nanibush

Roy Lloyd O'Halloran

Duncan Pegahmagabow

Merle Pegahmagabow

James Edward Wheatley

Index

Index

Credits

IT IS WITH GREAT PLEASURE that I acknowledge the assistance given to me during the years that I worked on this project.

First, this biography would not have been possible without the co-operation and trust of the late Duncan Pegahmagabow, who not only shared his memories but also gave me unlimited access to his father's letters and personal papers. Megwitch to Marie Anderson. Although she declined a 1990 request, Francis Pegahmagabow's last surviving child sat with me for several hours one day in 2005 to discuss her recollections of her father with often surprising frankness. As a result, many previously unknown things emerged about the life and character of Canada's most decorated First People's soldier.

I am grateful to Dr. Duane Hale of Cisco, Texas, for directing me to the Wanamaker Collection at Mathers Museum, Indiana University, and also to Wasauksing First Nation councillor Vincent Chechock for allowing me to come to his home to reproduce several photographs in the band's collection. I appreciated the assistance extended by National Archives of Canada archivist Bill Russell and by John Leslie of Indian Affairs in pointing out several archival sources that were unknown to me.

Thank you to the following who agreed to read early drafts of this manuscript and offered both their suggestions and encouragement: Dr. Donald Smith of the Department of History at the

University of Calgary; former Canadian War Museum historian Fred Gaffen; the late Franz Koennecke, author of the MA thesis "Wasoksing: The History of Parry Island, An Anishnabwe Community in the Georgian Bay, 1850–1920"; and John Macfie, whose father, Roy, served with Francis Pegahmagabow in the 1st Battalion, CEF. In 1990, Mr. Macfie published the book *Letters Home*, based on a collection of correspondence written by his father and two uncles while serving in the trenches.

Adrian Hayes with his daughter, Caitlin.

(photo by Jeanette Forsythe)

About the Author

ADRIAN HAYES is a journalist with a strong interest in history. His penchant for digging into the past to bring forward stories of interest and importance is reflected in his education: he holds degrees in both history and journalism.

His career in journalism began with the *Parry Sound North Star*, his hometown newspaper. In addition to covering news stories, Adrian wrote a local history column. In his research for that, he unearthed many fascinating stories, one of which formed the basis for his first published book, *Murder and Mayhem at Waubamik: The Shooting of Thomas Jackson* (2002).

It was also during this period that Adrian discovered more about the legendary Francis Pegahmagabow. Spending much time talking with First Nations people in the Parry Sound region, as well as searching archival records and conducting interviews farther afield, he amassed more information about the aboriginal corporal than anyone else had. He knew the story needed to be told. The result was his second book: the story of Canada's most decorated First Peoples soldier and his ongoing quest for civil rights and human dignity in the decades following the First World War.

In the meantime, Adrian came to know other Ontario communities as he advanced his journalism career, working as a reporter for *Orillia Today*, then the *Barrie Examiner*, and finally as managing editor of the *Uxbridge Times-Journal*. With his wife and daughter, he now lives in Newmarket and is currently employed by Transcontinental Publishing. Adrian is also author of the book *Parry Sound: Gateway to Northern Ontario* (2005).

More great reading from Blue Butterfly Books

If you enjoyed *Pegahmagabow: Life-long Warrior*, you might also like the following Blue Butterfly titles on related subjects. Your local bookseller can order any of them for you if they are not in stock, or you can order direct by going to the Blue Butterfly Books website:

www.bluebutterflybooks.ca

When impoverished, disheartened, poorly educated, but well-armed aboriginal young people find a modern revolutionary leader in the tradition of 1880s rebellion leader Louis Riel, they rally with a battle cry "Take Back the Land!" Coordinated attacks on Canada's strategic energy supply facilities soon have the armed forces scrambling and the country's leaders reeling.

Uprising: A Novel, by Douglas L. Bland
Hard cover / 6 × 9 in. / 507 pages
ISBN 978-1-926577-00-5 / $39.95
Features: author interview, maps

Three to a Loaf *is the page-turning drama of Rory Ferrall, a young Anglo-German Canadian smuggled into Germany during the First World War to discover the Imperial General Staff's top-secret plan to break the deadlock on the Western Front.*

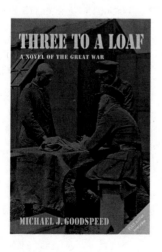

Three to a Loaf: A Novel of the Great War
by Michael J. Goodspeed
Soft cover / 6 × 9 in. / 365 pages
ISBN 978-0-9781600-6-7 / $24.95
Features: author interview

About this book

FRANCIS PEGAHMAGABOW was a remarkable aboriginal leader who served his nation in time of war and his people in time of peace—fighting all the way. In wartime he volunteered to be a warrior. In peacetime he had no option. His life reveals how uncaring Canada was about those to whom this land had always been home.

A member of the Parry Island band (now Wasauksing First Nation) near Parry Sound, Ontario, Francis served with the Canadian Expeditionary Force in Belgium and France for almost the entire duration of the First World War, primarily as a scout and sniper. Through the horrific battles and inhuman conditions of trench warfare, his actions earned him three decorations for bravery—the most ever received by a Canadian aboriginal soldier. More recently, they inspired the central fictional character in Joseph Boyden's highly acclaimed novel *Three Day Road*.

Physically and emotionally scarred by his wartime ordeals, Francis returned to Parry Island to try to rebuild his life. He had been treated as an equal in the army, but quickly discovered things hadn't changed back in Canada. As a status Indian his life was regulated by the infamous Indian Act and by local Indian agents who seemed bent on thwarting his every effort to improve his lot.

So, Francis became a warrior once more—this time in the even longer battle to achieve the right of aboriginal Canadians to control their own destiny.

In compiling this account of Francis Pegahmagabow's remarkable life, Adrian Hayes conducted extensive research in newspapers, archives, and military records, and spoke with members of Pegahmagabow's family and others who remembered the plight and the perseverance of this warrior.

Originally published by Fox Meadow Creations, *Pegahmagabow* emerges again in this new Blue Butterfly Books edition, which incorporates additional material and updates some aspects of this unforgettable story—and the confusion that still surrounds it.

Following the sudden end to her marriage, Meg Wilkinson, Canada's first woman veterinarian, leaves her practice in Halifax to seek the legendary working wolf-dogs of the Yukon. She arrives in Dawson City in 1897 just as the Klondike gold rush is beginning, discovering a unique aboriginal connection.

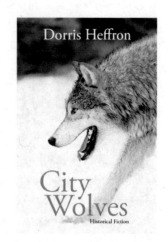

City Wolves: Historical Fiction
by Dorris Heffron
Hard or soft cover / 6 × 9 in. / 449 pages
ISBN (h.c.) 978-0-9781600-7-4 / $36.95
ISBN (s.c.) 978-1-926577-01-2 / $24.95
Features: author interview, maps

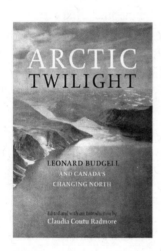

In a series of beautifully crafted letters, former Hudson's Bay Company "servant" Leonard Budgell describes the Canadian north from the 1920s to the 1980s, as could only be done by someone who lived and worked there. He documents an aboriginal way of life that was changing forever.

Arctic Twilight: Leonard Budgell and Canada's Changing North, edited and with an introduction by Claudia Coutu Radmore
Hard cover / 6 × 9 in. / 469 pages
ISBN 978-0-9781600-1-2 / $39.95
Features: photos, map, interview with editor

Blue Butterfly Books
THINK FREE, BE FREE
bluebutterflybooks.ca